THE CHEMICAL INDUSTRY

Selected Topics

R E Lee BSc

Stanley Thornes (Publishers) Ltd

© R E Lee 1988
Illustrations © Stanley Thornes (Publishers) Ltd 1988

All rights reserved. No part* of this publication may be reproduced, stored in a retrieval system or transmitted in any form or by any means, electronic, mechanical, photocopying, recording or otherwise, without the prior written consent of the copyright holders. Applications for such permission should be addressed to the publishers: Stanley Thornes (Publishers) Ltd, Old Station Drive, Leckhampton, CHELTENHAM GL53 0DN.

First published in 1988 by
Stanley Thornes (Publishers) Ltd
Old Station Drive
Leckhampton
CHELTENHAM
GL53 0DN

*An exception is made for the puzzles on pp. 25 and 64.
Teachers may photocopy a puzzle to save time for a pupil who would otherwise need to copy from his/her copy of the book. Teachers wishing to make multiple copies of a word puzzle for distribution to a class without individual copies of the book must apply to the publishers in the normal way.

British Library Cataloguing in Publication Data

Lee, R.E.
   The chemical industry.
   1. Chemical industries
   I. Title II. Series
   338.4'766

ISBN 0-85950-821-8

Typeset by Tech-Set, Gateshead, Tyne & Wear.
Printed and bound in Great Britain by Ebenezer Baylis & Son, Worcester.

CONTENTS

Preface iv

Chapter 1 Acids and alkalis worth their salt

Ammonia — a very important alkaline gas ... 2	Calcium carbonate — another important salt ... 18
Nitric acid ... 5	Activity 2 Making concrete and testing its strength ... 21
Sulphuric acid — yardstick of prosperity? ... 6	Activity 3 Glass-blowing ... 23
Sodium chloride — an important salt mined in the UK ... 9	Crossword ... 24
Activity 1 Making soap ... 13	Exercise ... 25
Sodium carbonate — glass-maker and much, much more ... 14	

Chapter 2 Drugs and dyes

What are drugs? ... 27	Dyes ... 35
How do drugs work? ... 27	The manufacture of a dye ... 37
How are new drugs developed? ... 29	Activity 5 Making Sudan Orange on a small scale ... 37
The top ten drugs in the world ... 33	Exercise ... 39
Opren ... 33	
The manufacture of penicillin ... 34	
Activity 4 To show antibiotic nature (antibiosis) ... 35	

Chapter 3 Liquid gold — to the chemist

How do they find the oil? ... 40	Alcohol to replace oil in the next century? ... 54
How do they get the oil out? ... 42	Making a modern petrol ... 55
North Sea oil and gas fields ... 44	A success story — the Mossmorran NGL pipeline ... 56
What does crude oil contain? ... 46	Coal — fuel of the future? ... 58
Separating oil into its useful parts ... 47	The modern coal mine ... 59
Fractional distillation ... 49	Chemicals from coal ... 59
Cracking ... 50	Activity 8 Destructive distillation of coal ... 60
Activity 6 Cracking medicinal paraffin ... 51	Fluidised-bed combustion ... 61
Reforming ... 51	Coal-powered cars ... 62
Other substances from oil ... 51	Exercise ... 63
Activity 7 Making a soapless detergent ... 52	Crossword ... 64
How does the world use oil? ... 53	

Chapter 4   How long is a molecule? — plastic polymers

Types of plastic	67
How are plastics made?	69
What do they do to plastics?	71
Additives to polymers	72
Biodegradable plastics	72
Activity 9 A project you could do	73
A success story — plastic waste back to oil	73
Data on plastics	74
Activity 10 Heat conductivity test	74
Exercise	75

Chapter 5   The farmer's friends — fertilisers and pesticides

What are fertilisers?	77
Activity 11 To show that powders may be granulated by the addition of a liquid	78
Why are fertilisers needed?	78
Do fertilisers really work?	79
Activity 12 The effect of nutrients on plant growth	79
Are fertilisers cost-effective?	80
Are there problems with fertilisers?	82
The farmer at war — the fight against pests	82
Making a pesticide	87
Concern about pesticides	88
Future control of pests	89
Exercise	90

Index	91
Acknowledgements	92
Answers to crosswords	92

PREFACE

I have written this book to give pupils a grasp of the huge contribution made to our lives by the chemical industry. It is an industry employing well over a quarter of a million people in the UK. As the UK's fourth biggest manufacturing industry, it is our top export earner.

The major chemical processes are included in this book. Over-use of chemical equations has been avoided as these often become a stumbling block to progress in chemistry. The book is intended to complement GCSE and Standard Grade courses involving chemistry. It should also be useful for modular (balanced) science courses that include 'materials and their uses' in the core or as an option. I make no apology for the extra detail given for selected chemical processes, since this should give a deeper insight into vital processes and indeed extend the pupils' understanding of science. The book will also be a useful general reader on the chemical industry. I hope that it will enthuse pupils enough for them to explore the possibility of a career in this vital industry.

Robert E. Lee
St George's College, Weybridge

CHAPTER 1
ACIDS AND ALKALIS WORTH THEIR SALT

Acids and alkalis can be dangerous. This is a simulated accident involving a tanker of acid. The acid is being transferred to another tanker. About 40 million tonnes of chemicals are distributed by road in the UK each year. About half of this material is hazardous to humans or animals

Some acids, on the other hand, are harmless. (These all contain acids.)

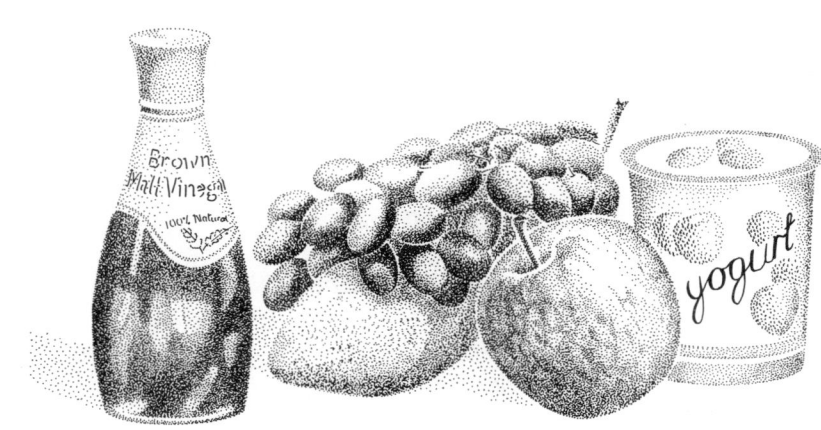

> **TRANSPORT EMERGENCY CARD (ROAD)**
>
> CEFIC TEC (R)-1
> April 1979 Rev. 3
> Class 2 ADR
> Item 3 at
>
> **Cargo**   **AMMONIA**   UN. No. 1005
> Liquefied pressure gas with pungent odour
>
> **Nature of Hazard**
> Corrosive and toxic
> Reaction with moist air produces mist which has strongly irritant effect on eyes, skin and air passages
> Contact with liquid causes skinburns
> Spilled liquid has very low temperature and, unless contained, evaporates quickly
>
> **Protective Devices**
> Suitable respiratory protective device
> Goggles giving complete protection to eyes
> Plastic or rubber gloves, boots, suit and hood givigg complete protection to head, face and neck
> Eyewash bottle with clean water
>
> **EMERGENCY ACTION** — Notify police and fire brigade immediately
> - If possible move vehicle to open ground
> - Stop the engine
> - Mark the roads and warn other road users
> - Keep public away from danger area
> - Keep upwind
> - Put on protective clothing
>
> **Spillage**
> - If vapour cloud drifts towards populated area, warn inhabitants
> - Contain leaking liquid with sand or earth; allow to evaporate
> - If this is not practicable use waterspray to "knock down" vapour
>
> **Fire**
> - Keep containers cool by spraying with water if exposed to fire
>
> **First aid**
> - If the substance has got into the eyes, immediately wash out with plenty of water for at least 15 minutes
> - Remove contaminated clothing immediately and wash affected skin with plenty of water
> - Seek medical treatment when anyone has symptoms apparently due to inhalation or contact with skin or eyes
> - Persons who have inhaled the gas must lie down and keep quite still
> - Keep patient warm,
> - Do not apply artificial respiration if patient is breathing
>
> Additional information provided by manufacturer or sender
> Forwarded by IMPERIAL CHEMICAL INDUSTRIES PLC
> AGRICULTURAL DIVISION, PO Box 8, BILLINGHAM, CLEVELAND, TS23 1LB
> **TELEPHONE** EMERGENCY — STOCKTON-ON-TEES (0642) 553768
>
> Prepared by CEFIC (CONSEIL EUROPEEN DES FEDERATIONS DE L'INDUSTRIE CHIMIQUE, EUROPEAN COUNCIL OF CHEMICAL MANUFACTURERS' FEDERATIONS) Zürich, from the best knowledge available; no responsibility is accepted that the information is sufficient or correct in all cases
> Acknowledgment is made to V.N.C.I. and E.V.O. of the Netherlands for their help in the preparation of this card
>
> Applies only during road Transport   English

TREMCARD carried in all vehicle cabs to alert public emergency services on procedures to be adopted if an accident occurs

There are many acids, both weak and strong, in common use. Alkalis are chemical 'opposites' of acids. There are very few commonly used alkalis. These are sodium hydroxide, potassium hydroxide, aqueous ammonia (sometimes called ammonium hydroxide) and calcium hydroxide. Aqueous ammonia is used in the home to 'cut through' the grease around sinks and baths. Ammonia gas is also alkaline and a most important industrial compound.

AMMONIA — A VERY IMPORTANT ALKALINE GAS

Ammonia (formula NH_3) has many important uses. Eighty per cent of all ammonia produced is used to make fertilisers. Other main uses are for making polymers (p. 66) such as nylon and polyurethane, dyes and explosives. Nitric acid is manufactured from ammonia, air and water.

World ammonia production, 1910–80

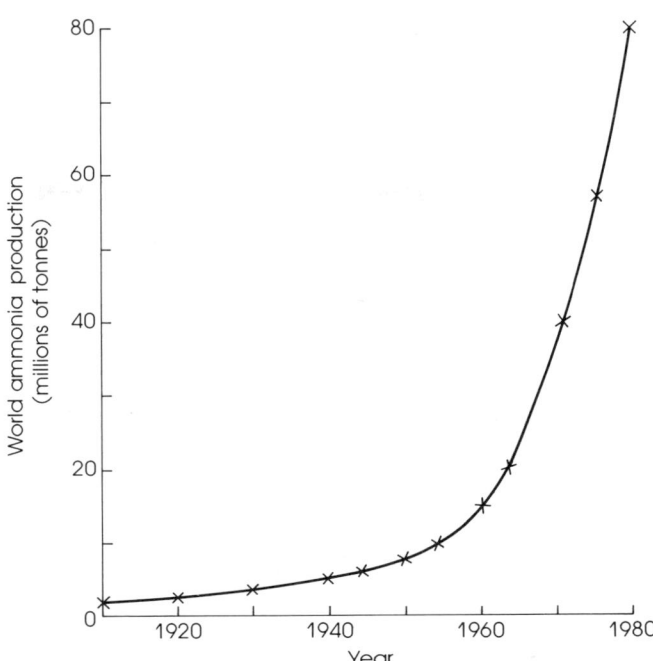

Look at the graph of world ammonia production and answer these questions:

- State the years over which there was a small gradual increase in production of ammonia.
- In which year, approximately, did a sudden rise in ammonia production start?
- What factors do you think contributed to this sudden rise?
- Compare the production of ammonia for 1970 with that for 1980.

Ammonia is made from its elements, nitrogen and hydrogen. Making a compound from its elements is called *synthesis*. Ammonia is made by the *Haber process*, named after the German chemist who invented it. The hydrogen used to be made by passing steam over red-hot coke:

Steam + Coke ⇌ Carbon monoxide + Hydrogen
H_2O + C ⇌ CO + H_2

The modern way to get the hydrogen is from hydrocarbons such as natural gas:

Methane + Steam → Carbon dioxide + Hydrogen
CH_4 + $2H_2O$ → CO_2 + $4H_2$

A nickel *catalyst* is necessary to make this reaction fast enough to be useful. A catalyst is a substance that changes the rate of a chemical reaction without being changed itself.

The naphtha fraction of crude oil (p. 49) can also be used in a similar way to natural gas. Whichever hydrocarbon is used, hydrogen sulphide gas must be removed because this would 'poison' the catalyst. The nitrogen for the Haber process comes from air.

Look at the chart below, which compares the use of coke with that of hydrocarbons to make the hydrogen for the Haber process.

Differences between coke- and hydro-carbon-based ammonia plants (1974 figures)

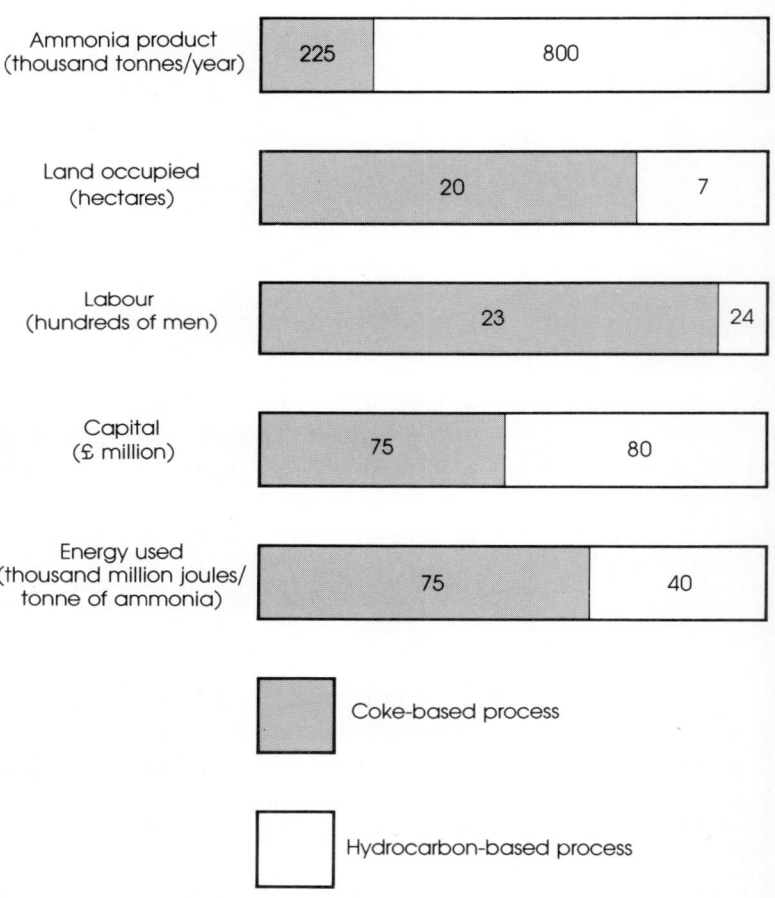

- Which of the processes requires fewer workers?
- Which of the processes requires less land?
- Which of the processes requires less energy?
- Which factor is similar for both processes?
- Which of the processes is producing the more ammonia?

The Haber process

The equation for the process is:

Nitrogen + Hydrogen ⇌ Ammonia
$$N_2 + 3H_2 \rightleftharpoons 2NH_3$$

Note that it is a reversible reaction. It is possible for ammonia to split up to form nitrogen and hydrogen, so in the process conditions are chosen that make nitrogen and hydrogen combine as quickly as possible compared with the reverse reaction. This results in a mixture containing 15 per cent ammonia, which is extracted, and the unused nitrogen and hydrogen are recycled.

Roughly 7000 tonnes of liquid ammonia are produced each day in the UK as the total from seven different chemical plants.

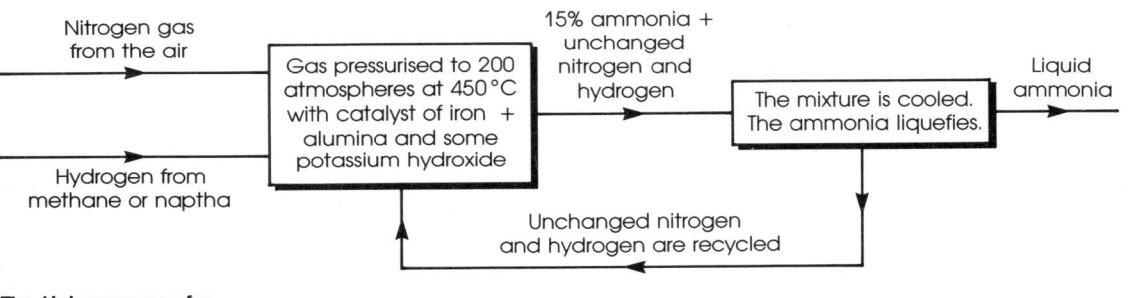

The Haber process for ammonia manufacture

NITRIC ACID

Nitric acid (formula HNO_3) is important in chemistry for making:
 Nitrates, e.g. ammonium nitrate (fertiliser, explosive and source of 'laughing gas')
 Explosives
 Fertilisers
 Dyes
 Plastics

Nitric acid manufacture

The flow chart for this process is shown on the next page. The word equation for the process is:

Ammonia + Air + Water → Nitric acid

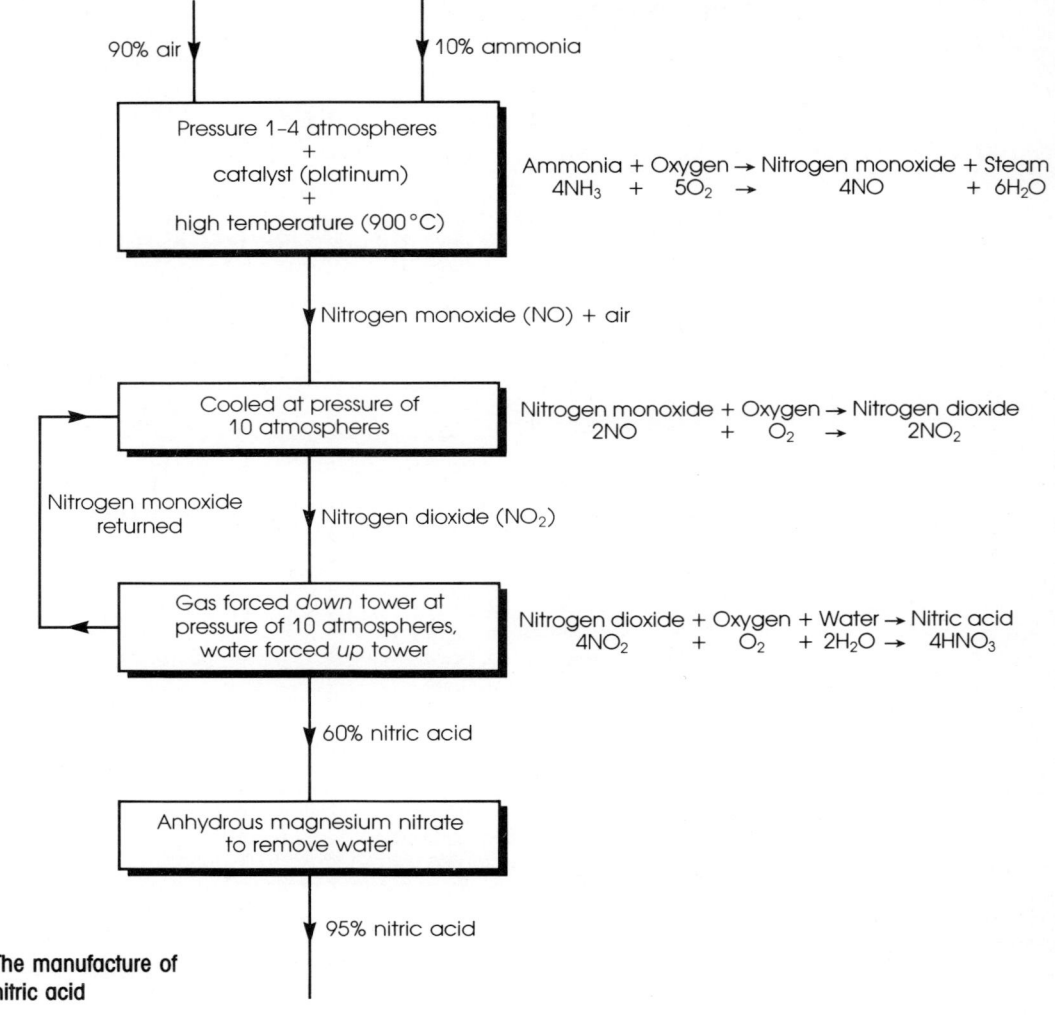

The manufacture of nitric acid

SULPHURIC ACID — YARDSTICK OF PROSPERITY?

Sulphuric acid is used at some stage in the production of most of the goods that we buy. The graph shows how the average amount of sulphuric acid used daily in the UK varied over a period of about ten years. The demand for sulphuric acid varies according to the quantity of goods being manufactured, and so in the past has been taken as a rough measure of the country's prosperity. Today, however, the consumption of chlorine is perhaps a better measure, because it is used in the manufacture of many of the substances so evident in modern life.

Sulphuric acid is manufactured almost wholly by the *Contact process* today. The USA and USSR are the major producers, with the UK producing only 2 per cent of the world output.

Sulphuric acid consumption in the UK

UK consumption (tonnes/day)
11 000
10 000
9000
8000
7000
6000
1973
'74
'75
'76
'77
'78
'79
'80
'81
'82
'83
Year

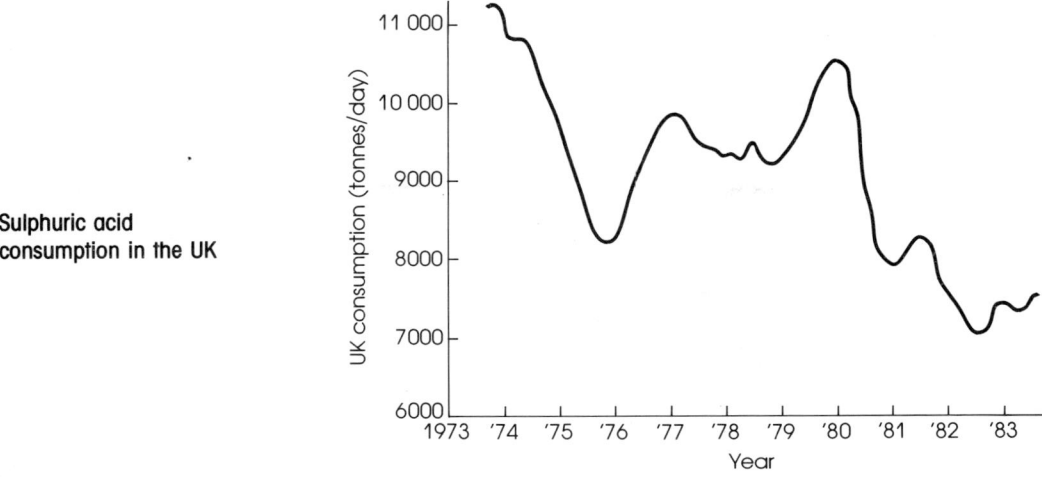

A flow chart for the process is shown below.

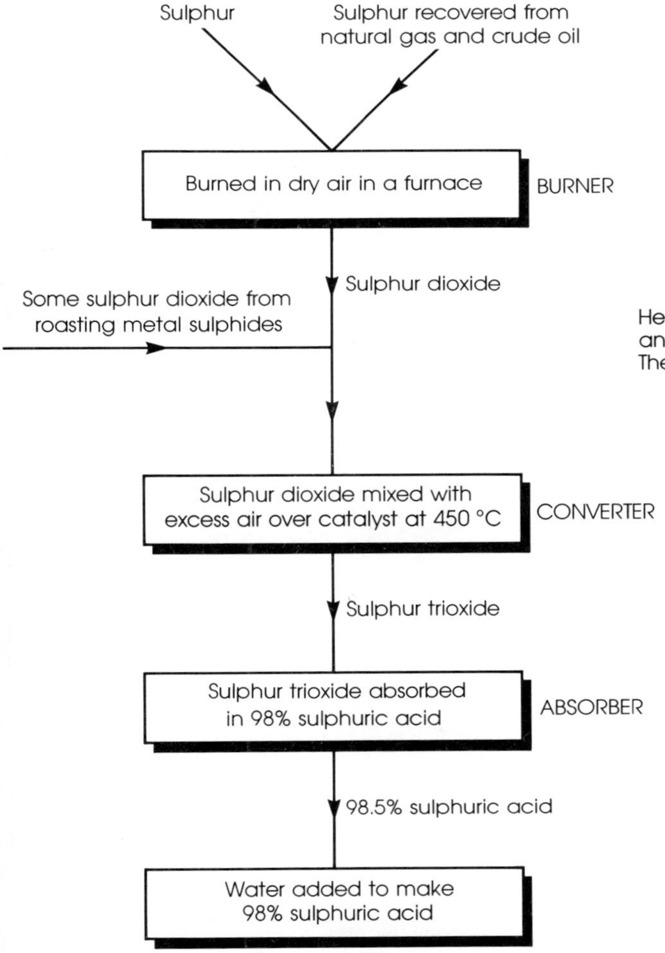
Sulphur
Sulphur recovered from natural gas and crude oil
Burned in dry air in a furnace
BURNER
Sulphur dioxide
Some sulphur dioxide from roasting metal sulphides
Sulphur dioxide mixed with excess air over catalyst at 450 °C
CONVERTER
Sulphur trioxide
Sulphur trioxide absorbed in 98% sulphuric acid
ABSORBER
98.5% sulphuric acid
Water added to make 98% sulphuric acid

Sulphur + Oxygen → Sulphur dioxide

$S + O_2 \rightarrow SO_2$

Heat is given out at each stage and is used to convert water into steam. The steam is sold.

Sulphur dioxide + Oxygen ⇌ Sulphur trioxide

$2SO_2 + O_2 \rightleftharpoons 2SO_3$

Sulphur trioxide + Concentrated sulphuric acid → Fuming sulphuric acid (oleum)

$SO_3 + H_2SO_4 \rightarrow H_2S_2O_7$

Oleum + Water → Concentrated sulphuric acid

$H_2S_2O_7 + H_2O \rightarrow 2H_2SO_4$

The Contact process

Why choose Merseyside for a chemical factory?

A sulphuric acid plant should be near its major customers; otherwise transport costs make it unworthwhile. Sulphur has to be imported, and so the plant must be near trains and/or a major shipping port. There must also be enough skilled workers in the area, and the factory must be close to customers who need the steam. Such is the ICI plant at Runcorn in Cheshire.

Look at the following maps and use them to answer the questions. Write an essay on why the area is well suited for a chemical factory.

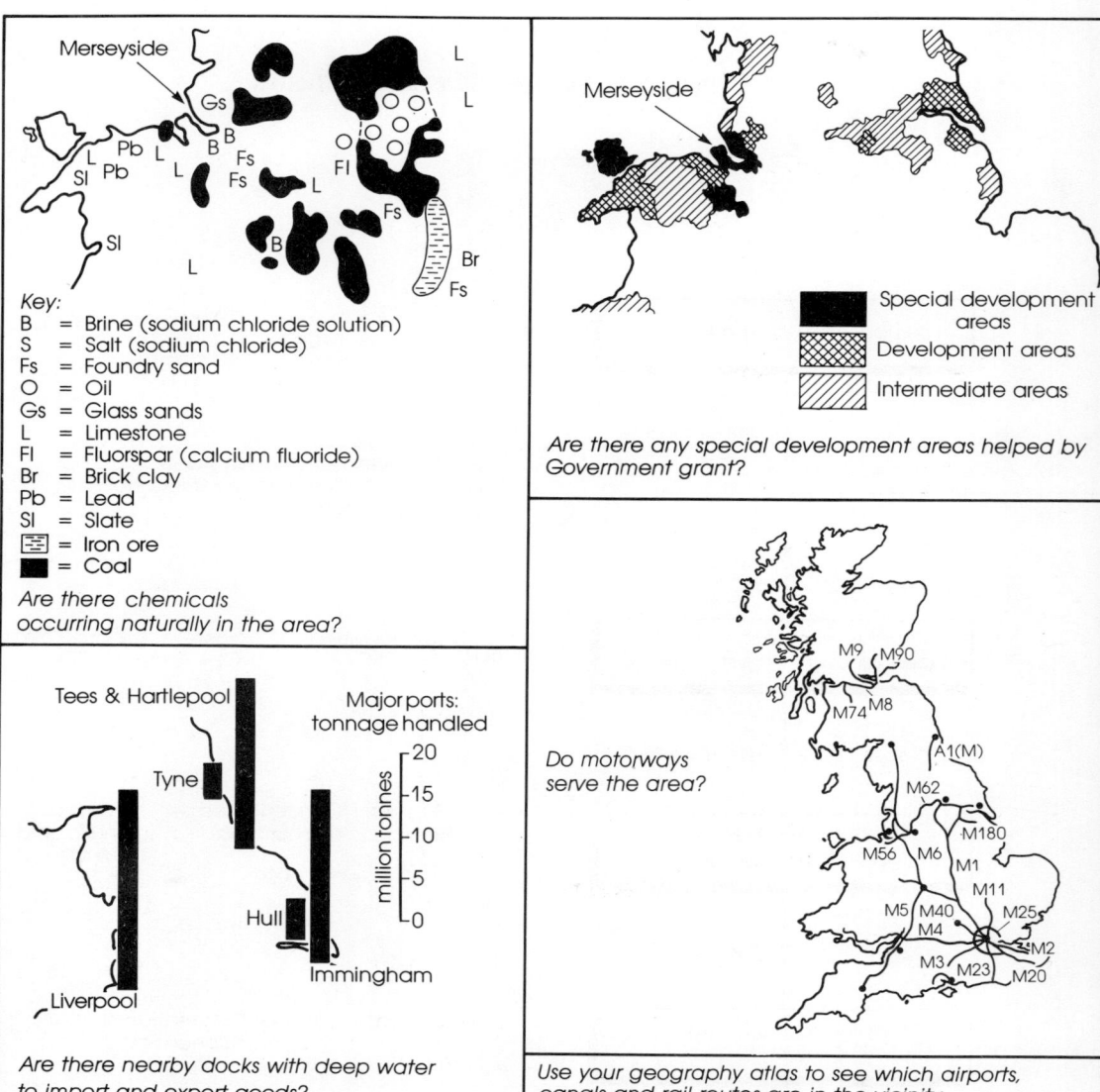

Key:
B = Brine (sodium chloride solution)
S = Salt (sodium chloride)
Fs = Foundry sand
O = Oil
Gs = Glass sands
L = Limestone
Fl = Fluorspar (calcium fluoride)
Br = Brick clay
Pb = Lead
Sl = Slate
= Iron ore
= Coal

Are there chemicals occurring naturally in the area?

Are there any special development areas helped by Government grant?

Are there nearby docks with deep water to import and export goods?

Do motorways serve the area?

Use your geography atlas to see which airports, canals and rail routes are in the vicinity.
There must also be enough skilled workers in the area.

Uses of sulphuric acid

Over 3.4 million tonnes of sulphuric acid are used in the UK each year. Use the figures below to construct your own bar graph of UK usage of sulphuric acid:

Use	Percentage
Fertiliser/agricultural	30.4
Chemicals	16.4
Paints/pigments	15.7
Detergents/soaps	11.7
Natural and synthetic fibres	9.4
Work with metals	2.3
Dyes	2.0
Oil/petrol	1.0
Other uses	11.1

SODIUM CHLORIDE — AN IMPORTANT SALT MINED IN THE UK

The UK supply of sodium chloride comes from mining 'rock salt' at ICI plants in Cheshire. At Nantwich the common salt is brought to the surface by dissolving it in water. This *solution mining* gives pure salt. At Winsford the common salt is brought to the surface by *cavity* and *pillar mining*. Rock salt obtained in this way is impure and is used on the roads to prevent icy patches. Some hot countries get their supply of this salt by evaporating sea-water. The sea-water salt contains other salts too.

Cavity mining

Solution mining

- Look at a map of Cheshire. You will see Nantwich, Middlewich and Northwich. 'Nant' means 'south'. What do you think 'wich' means?
- Explain how salt can be brought to the surface using water. Would this method work for other minerals?

Sodium chloride is important, not only because it has many uses itself, but also because so many other important chemicals can be made from it. The diagram below shows some of its uses.

Uses of sodium chloride

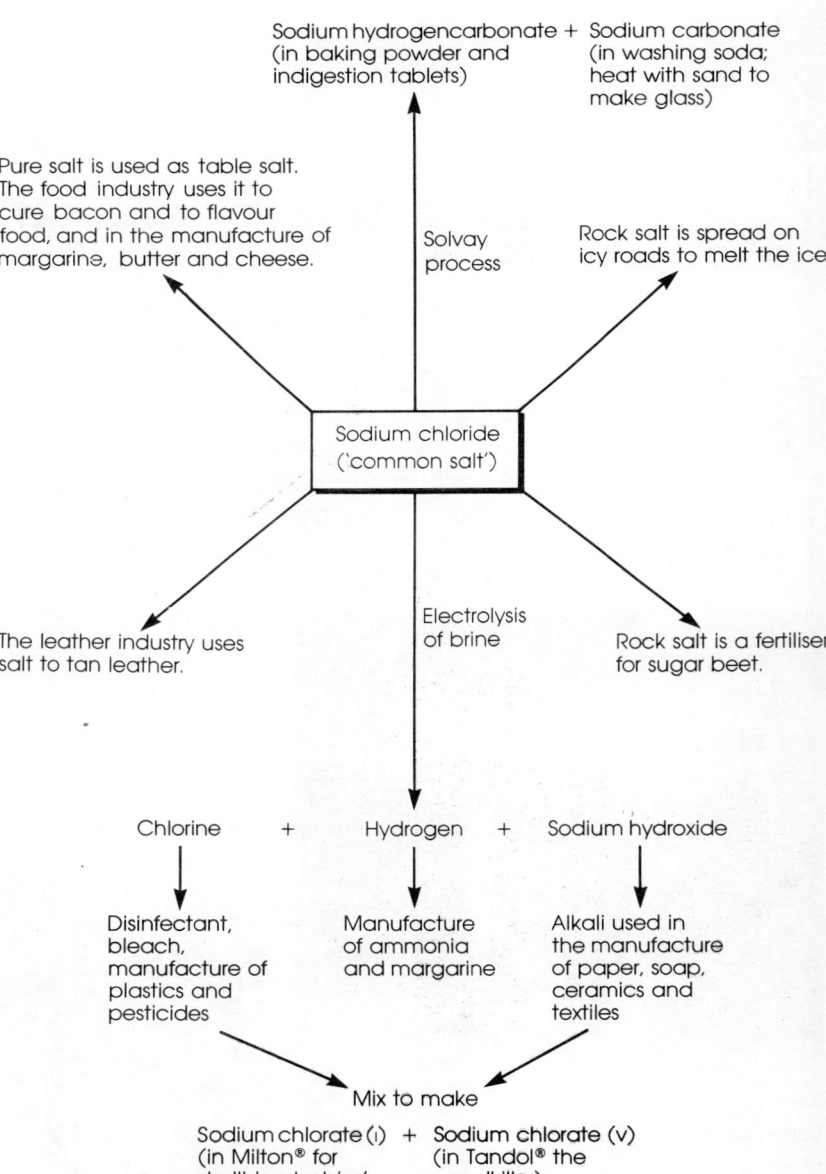

The chlor-alkali industry

The chlor-alkali industry is based on sodium chloride and water. It is one of the most important branches of chemical manufacturing. There are three industrial methods for converting sodium chloride into sodium hydroxide and chlorine. All of them involve passing an electric current through sodium chloride solution (brine). Sodium chloride contains sodium ions (Na^+) and chloride ions (Cl^-). These ions are attracted to the electrodes by applying a voltage to the solution. The sodium ions go to the negatively charged electrode (the cathode) and the chloride ions go to the positively charged electrode (the anode). At the electrodes the charges on the ions are neutralised, and the elements sodium and chlorine are produced. This breakdown of sodium chloride using electricity is called *electrolysis*.

The mercury cell is one of the important methods of converting brine into sodium hydroxide and chlorine.

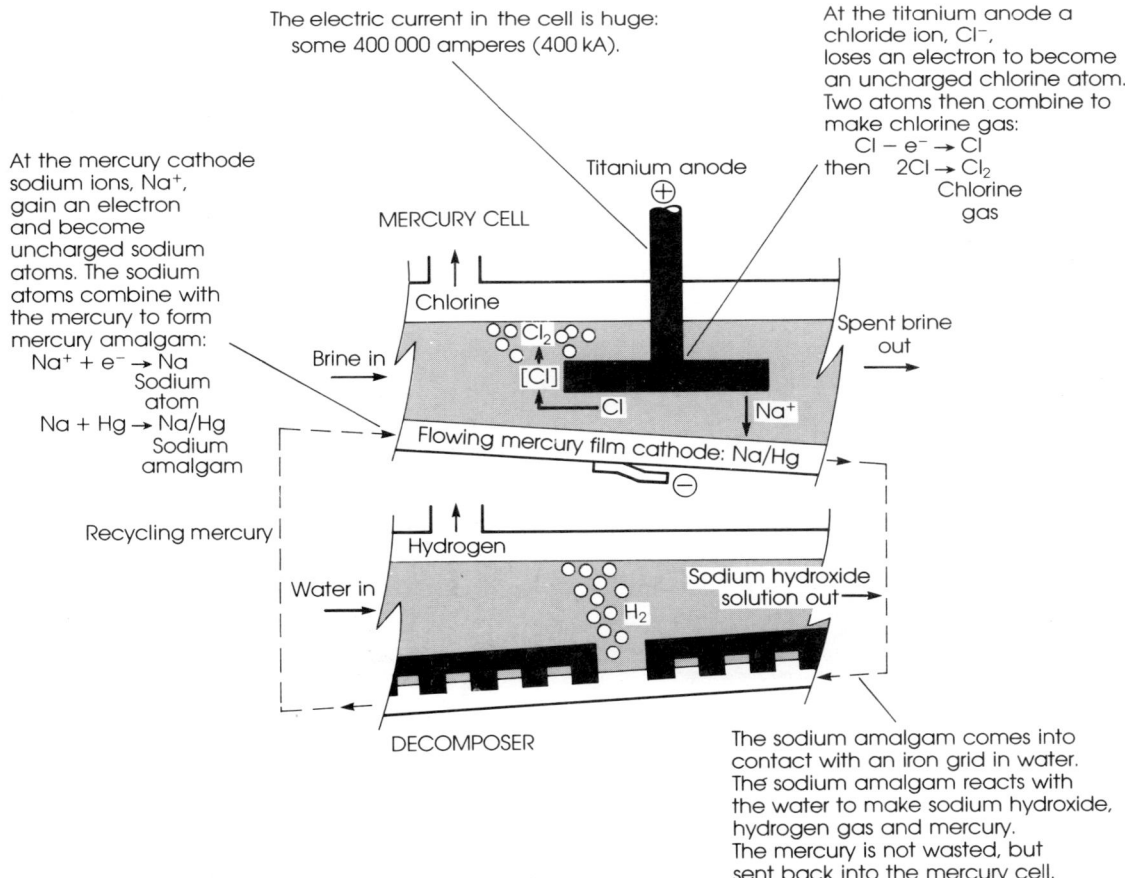

Mercury cell for making sodium hydroxide

Western Europe consumed about 9 million tonnes of both sodium hydroxide and chlorine in 1983. The major uses of these chemicals are summarised below. Construct pie charts to illustrate these figures:

Chlorine	%
Organic chlorine compounds	62
Making the plastic, PVC	30
Paper making	4
Water treatment	4

Sodium Hydroxide	%
Making sodium compounds	50
Textiles	8
Paper making	8
Soaps	7
Purifying metal ores (aluminium)	5
Water treatment	4
Food	2
Others	16

Soap manufacture

Sodium hydroxide is vital to the soap-making industry. The basic process is:

Fat or oil + Sodium hydroxide → Soap + Glycerol
(glycerine)

The stages of manufacture are shown in the following flow chart.

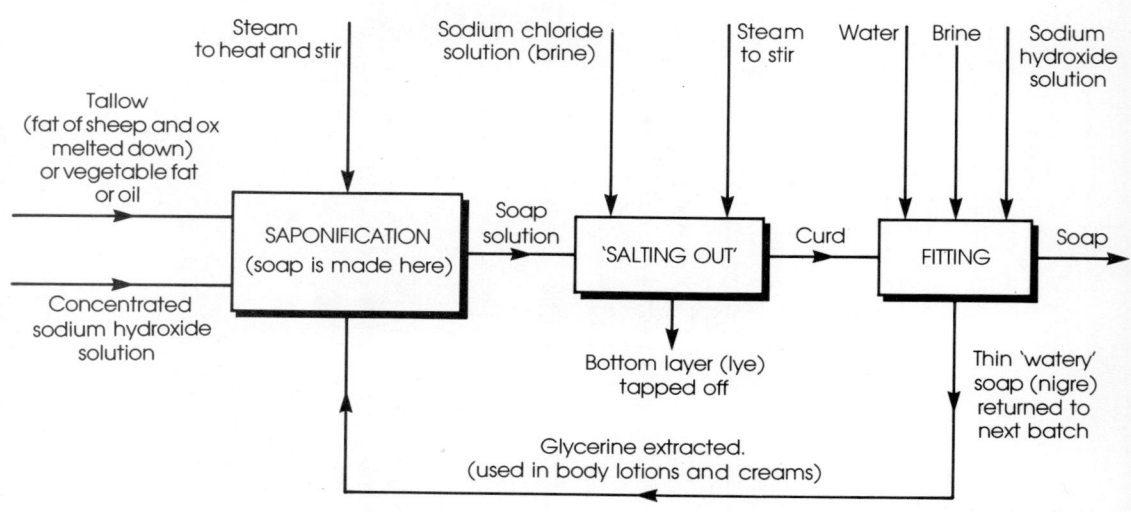

The manufacture of soap

ACTIVITY 1

Making soap

1) Pour 5 cm³ of castor oil into a boiling-tube. Add 25 cm³ of sodium hydroxide solution (concentration 4 moles per litre) to the castor oil. Place the boiling-tube in the beaker of water. WEAR SAFETY GLASSES throughout this experiment: you are using a hot, concentrated alkali.

2) Boil the water in the beaker for about twenty minutes. The steam will heat the mixture in the boiling-tube. Stir the mixture throughout this heating stage.

3) Transfer the mixture from the boiling-tube to a beaker. Add 25 cm³ of a saturated solution of sodium chloride to the beaker. Bring the mixture to the boil, adding colouring if desired. The soap should form a frothy top layer.

4) Add any perfume required to the mixture. Allow the mixture to cool. Remove the cake of soap from the cold mixture. The cake should be broken up and washed to remove trapped sodium hydroxide. Filter off the soap. Heat the soap and pour it into a mould.

Synthetic detergents: better than soap?

Ordinary soap is made from animal fats. Soap has some disadvantages for washing clothes in that it forms a scum in hard-water areas. This sticks to the clothes. Soap also works poorly in acid conditions, so if the dirt makes the water acidic, the soap does not clean properly.

Detergents are present in washing powders and liquids, dish-washing powders, hard surface cleaners, scouring powders, shampoos and so-called liquid soaps. Other chemicals are added to the detergent to increase efficiency. These are known as *builders*. These are mainly compounds of sodium:

- *Sodium tripolyphosphate* softens the water.
- *Sodium silicate* keeps soil-dirt suspended in the water.
- *Sodium perborate* bleaches to make the fabric look cleaner.
- *Sodium sulphate* makes the detergent flow freely from the packet.

Of these the phosphate compound is now being replaced because waste water containing it acts as a fertiliser, and chokes rivers and lakes by encouraging too much plant growth.

Other chemicals are also added to give a whiter appearance, colouring and perfume.

One of the simplest ways of making a detergent comprises just two stages:

1) The diesel oil and kerosine fractions from crude oil (p. 49) are further distilled. The hydrocarbons with roughly twelve carbon atoms per molecule are collected.

2) Sulphur dioxide and oxygen are allowed to react with the hydrocarbons. Ultraviolet light is used to help the reaction. An alkane sulphonate detergent is formed.

Alkanes (12 carbon atoms) + Oxygen + Sulphur dioxide → Alkane sulphonates

Further information on soaps and detergents, together with some experiments you can do with them, may be found in *Extending Science 2: Water* by E N Ramsden and R E Lee (ST(P)).

SODIUM CARBONATE — GLASS-MAKER AND MUCH, MUCH MORE

Sodium carbonate is a salt which makes an alkaline solution. It is in great demand, 29 million tonnes being used each year. Sodium carbonate is often called 'soda ash' because centuries ago it was extracted from the ash of burnt plants. Soda ash has been used since ancient times to make glass.

Two types of sodium carbonate are manufactured. They differ in particle size. The lighter-particle version is called 'light ash' and the other 'heavy ash'. The ICI factory in mid-Cheshire makes one million tonnes of sodium carbonate each year, two-thirds of it being heavy ash. The two pie charts below show the various uses of the two types.

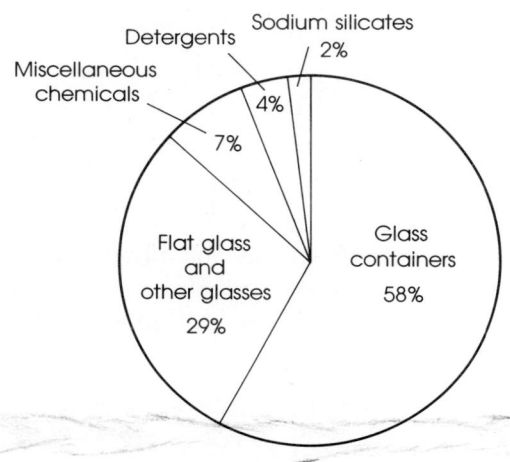

Major uses of heavy ash

Major uses of light ash

Pie chart:
- Other uses e.g. rubber and textiles 10%
- Detergents 15%
- Chemicals 50%
- Metal refining 25%

- Which type of ash is used for glass making?
- What percentage of this ash is used for glass making?
- Glass-makers' sand has a similar density and particle size to one type of ash. Which one do you think this is? How could similar density and particle size help in making glass?
- Which major use can involve light or heavy ash?
- What are the three most important uses for light ash?

The Solvay process (ammonia-soda process)

The manufacture of sodium carbonate involves many stages, but two chemical equations can sum up what happens. The important chemicals are sodium chloride, water, carbon dioxide gas and ammonia gas:

Sodium chloride + Ammonia + Water + Carbon dioxide

$NaCl + NH_3 + H_2O + CO_2$

⇌ Ammonium chloride + Sodium hydrogencarbonate

⇌ $NH_4Cl + NaHCO_3$

The sodium hydrogencarbonate is then simply heated:

Sodium hydrogencarbonate → Sodium carbonate + Water + Carbon dioxide

$2NaHCO_3 \rightarrow Na_2CO_3 + H_2O + CO_2$

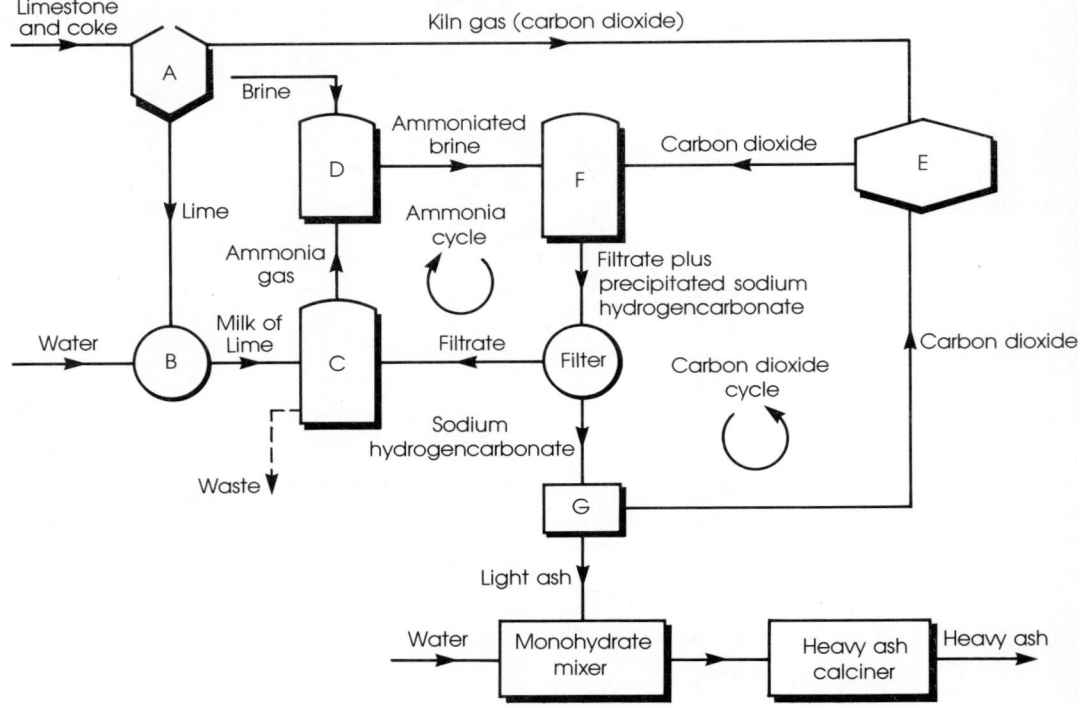

The Solvay process

The various parts of the chemical plant are as shown in the flow chart, and the processes that take place in them are as follows:

The Lime Kiln (A). Limestone (calcium carbonate) is mixed with coke and heated here. The coke burns, which raises the temperature to 1350 °C, and breaks the limestone down into calcium oxide (lime) and carbon dioxide:

Calcium carbonate → Calcium oxide + Carbon dioxide
(limestone)   (lime)
$CaCO_3$ → CaO + CO_2

If the flow chart of the Solvay process is followed, it can be seen that the lime kiln provides both the carbon dioxide and the lime for the process.

The Lime Dissolver (B). The lime is dissolved in water to make 'milk of lime'.

The Distiller (C). The 'milk of lime' (calcium hydroxide) is mixed with a salt, ammonium chloride, and heated. Ammonia gas distils off.

The Absorber (D). A concentrated solution of sodium chloride (brine) is passed down the absorber and ammonia gas is passed up. The brine dissolves the ammonia, making what is called 'ammoniated brine'. Some carbon dioxide is also bubbled into the ammoniated brine.

The Compressor (E). Carbon dioxide from the lime kiln is compressed to about 3 atmospheres of pressure.

The Solvay Tower (F). This is where the main reaction takes place. Ammoniated brine passes down the Solvay tower whilst carbon dioxide passes up it. The mixture reacts and sodium hydrogencarbonate crystals separate out at the cooled lower part of the tower. The temperature at which the crystals form is critical because the crystals must be big enough to be filtered off when they leave the tower. The sodium hydrogencarbonate crystals are washed and dried.

The Calciner (G). The calciner is a rotating drum heated by steam tubes. The sodium hydrogencarbonate changes to sodium carbonate during this heating. Carbon dioxide is given off, and this passes to the compressor to react again in the Solvay tower.

Heavy ash is made by adding a limited amount of water to the light ash, then heating this in the calciner.

Little is wasted: if you look at the flow chart it becomes obvious that most chemicals formed in the various stages are used. Two other useful substances formed are:

- Ammonium chloride. This is formed by treating the filtrate from the Solvay tower with more ammonia and sodium chloride. It is used in dry batteries and in metal processing.
- Calcium chloride. The waste liquid in the distiller is reduced in volume by evaporation and cooled. The less soluble salts crystallise out, leaving a concentrated solution of calcium chloride. When cooled, this solution gives calcium chloride crystals. Calcium chloride is used for refrigeration, making concrete, soil treatment, and in oil-drilling suspensions.

All chemical factories, however, pose some problems for the environment:

- Noise, caused by the handling of chemicals before and after the process.
- Pollution of the atmosphere by the sulphur dioxide from burning fuel. It can be minimised by using low-sulphur fuels or removing the sulphur dioxide chemically.
- Warm water, which is emptied into rivers, upsetting the balance of life in the river. This upset is minimised by recycling the water.

- Chemical waste. Any waste calcium hydroxide solution from the Solvay process is neutralised by hydrochloric acid before being stored in lagoons. The neutralised liquid is later passed to the river.

CALCIUM CARBONATE — ANOTHER IMPORTANT SALT

A chalk quarry

The UK supply of calcium carbonate comes from mining limestone and chalk, both of which are abundant in Britain. Calcium carbonate is useful both in itself and for the other chemicals that it makes. It is heated at 1000 °C in a lime kiln to make calcium oxide (lime).

Calcium carbonate → Calcium oxide + Carbon dioxide
$CaCO_3$ → CaO + CO_2

The calcium oxide formed is used to make sodium carbonate, glass and calcium hydroxide (slaked lime). Mortar, vital for holding bricks together in buildings, is made by mixing calcium hydroxide with sand and water. Cement and concrete are also made from calcium carbonate. These surround us in buildings, bridges, motorways and paths.

Calcium hydroxide has many uses, e.g.

- Neutralising acid soil
- Softening temporary hard water
- Making calcium hydrogensulphite for paper making
- Making bleaching powder
- 'Whitewash' for buildings

- Making mortar (by mixing one part calcium hydroxide with three parts sand)
- The Solvay process
- Recovering ammonia from the liquid obtained by heating coal (gasworks liquor)

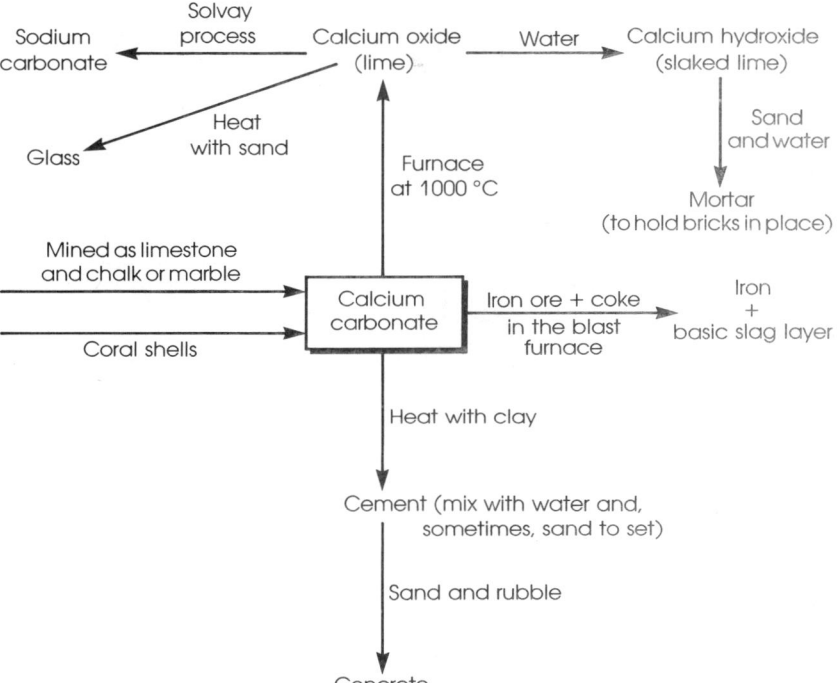

Uses of calcium carbonate

Limestone: a concrete use

Cement is made by heating a mixture of limestone, clay and water. The details are as follows:

1) The limestone and clay are crushed, ground and blended with water.

2) The mixture is heated close to its melting point (about 1400 °C) in a rotating kiln, which is fired by oil, natural gas or powdered coal. The product is large lumps called *clinker*.

3) The clinker is mixed with gypsum (calcium sulphate) and the two are ground together to a powder. The gypsum controls the setting time for the cement when it is used.

The end product is cement powder, which is sold for making mortar for bricklaying or for making concrete.

A concrete mixer

Concrete is made by mixing gravel, sand, cement and water. On a large scale this is done in a rotating mixer. After mixing, the concrete can be poured out and left to set. It is a strong material because the crystals of cement bind the sand and gravel together.

A modern example of concrete engineering: the new Thames Barrier protects London from serious tidal flooding

Cement to replace plastics and metals?

Cement is less strong and less tough than most plastics and most metals. A 3 mm thick sample of cement can be broken by hand and shatters when dropped to the floor. Plastics and metals would not shatter in the same way.

Scientists set about improving the properties of cement. They decided this could be done by reducing the size of the holes in the solid cement. They succeeded in reducing the hole size by:

- Increasing the power of the mixing machines
- Cutting down on the air that gets into cement
- Adding a chemical which stopped the particles from clinging together and thus getting bigger. The smaller the particles, the smaller the holes in the solid cement.

(a) 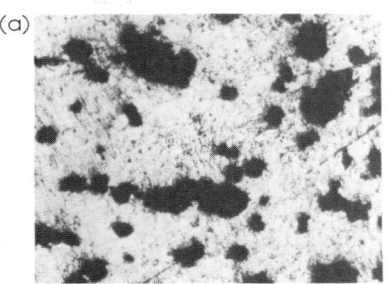 (b)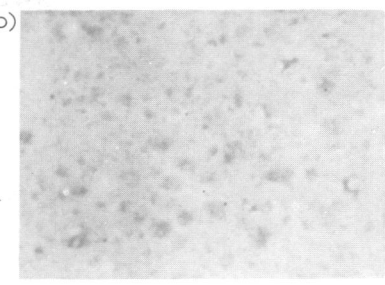

Polished cross-section of (a) ordinary cement, showing the large black holes in the structure, (b) the new cement, showing the large reduction in hole size

The scientists were amazed by the resulting cement. The properties matched those of plastics and metals. The new cement required less energy to make than do plastics and metals. It was superior to plastics in that it did not burn. The picture shows bottle caps made of the new cement. Watch out, plastics! Watch out, metals! You have a competitor made from simple and widely available chemicals.

Cement bottle caps

ACTIVITY 2

Making concrete and testing its strength

1) Look at the instructions for making concrete shown on a cement packet from your DIY shop. These should tell you the parts by weight of cement, sand and water to mix.

2) Weigh out these parts. Mix the ingredients and allow to set in a plastic yoghurt pot. Allow the concrete to set and remove it by breaking the pot if necessary.

3) Repeat the experiment, varying the parts by weight each time.

4) Devise a method for testing the strength of the concrete. Which mixture is the strongest?

A potential hazard

Cement works can produce vast quantities of dust, which coats everything in the area. The dust can also cause bronchial troubles. It is therefore desirable that a cement works produces as little dust as possible. It is very difficult to surround a working machine with a dust-tight box. Usually the air pressure in the box is reduced so that air flows in instead of out; this way the dust does not get into the air.

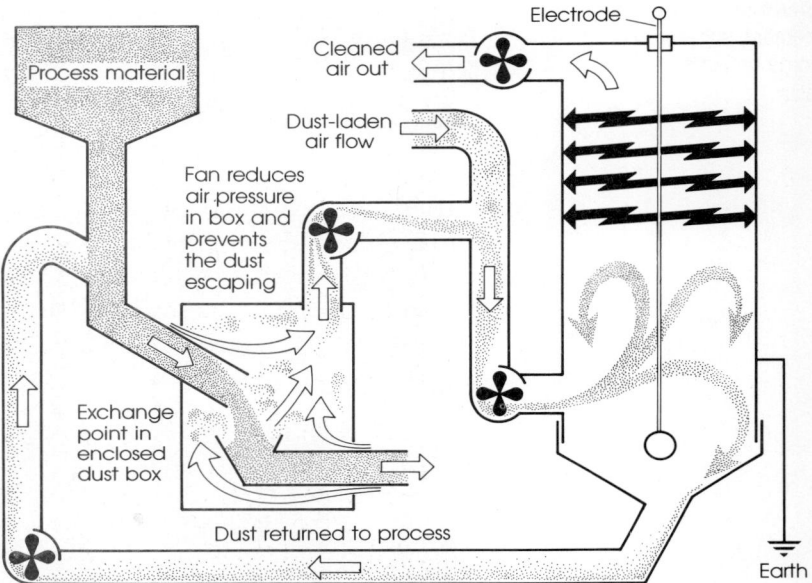

Electrostatic precipitator

The biggest dust cleaner is an electrostatic precipitator, as shown in the diagram. Dust-laden air passes between electrodes at 50 000 volts and earthed collecting plates. The dust particles get charged themselves and stick to the earthed plates. The dust can be removed safely and recycled into the process. This is a general method to remove harmful dust generated in a factory process.

From sandpits to glass—a salty connection

Common salt (sodium chloride) is converted to the salt sodium carbonate in the Solvay process. If sodium carbonate, limestone and sand are heated to about 800 °C they form glass. A typical recipe for glass is:

15 parts sand (silicon dioxide)
 5 parts sodium carbonate
 4 parts limestone

To the mixture is added 15 to 30 per cent scrap (recycled) glass. This saves on the energy required and helps to preserve raw materials as well as reducing the nuisance and danger of glass disposal. The limestone is used to produce an insoluble glass. In practice small amounts of other substances such as lead salts are added to the molten glass to alter its properties.

Glass melts easily and becomes treacly. It can be drawn into rods, rolled into sheets, moulded or blown.

Think of all the uses for glass and for concrete. Write an essay on life without these two materials. How would we cope? Life would certainly be very different.

ACTIVITY 3

Glass-blowing

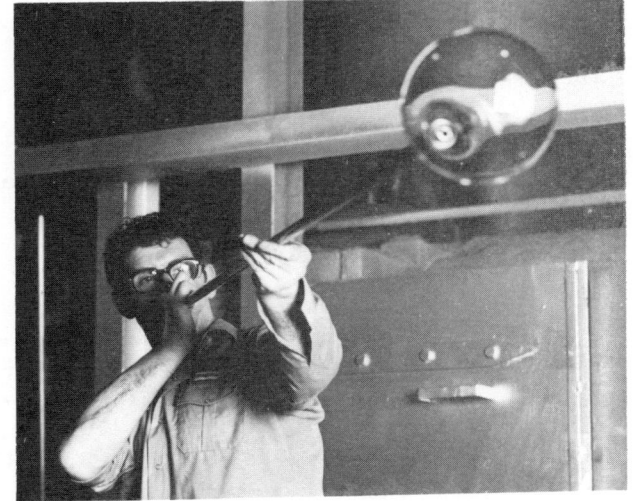

A professional glass-blower

You too can blow glass — but MAKE SURE YOU WEAR GOGGLES AND TAKE CARE.

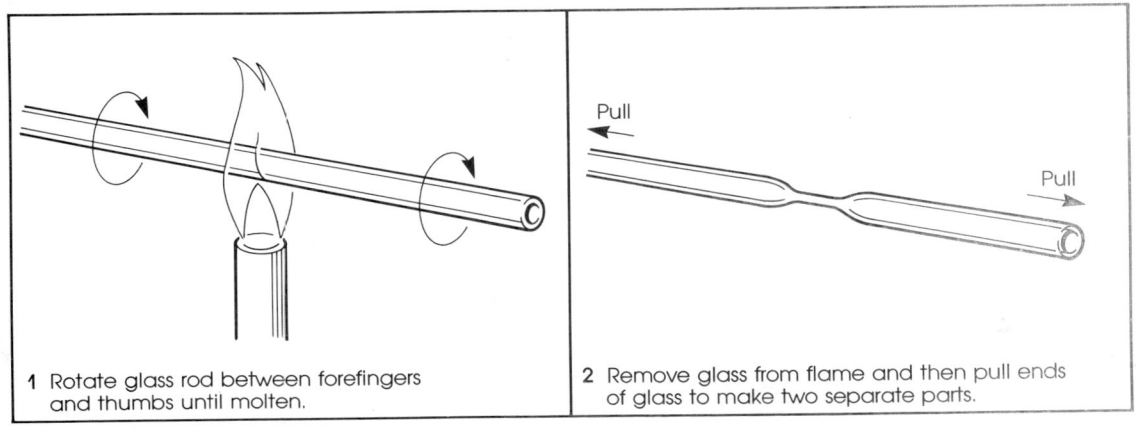

1 Rotate glass rod between forefingers and thumbs until molten.

2 Remove glass from flame and then pull ends of glass to make two separate parts.

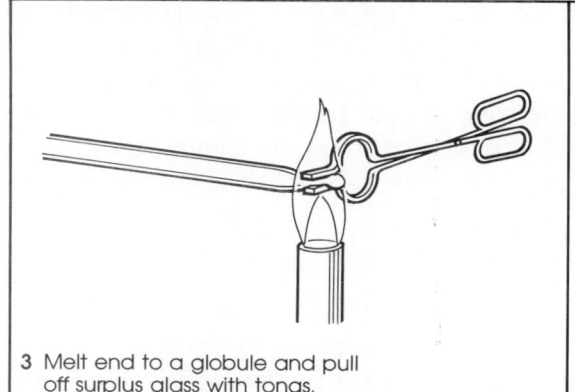

3 Melt end to a globule and pull off surplus glass with tongs.

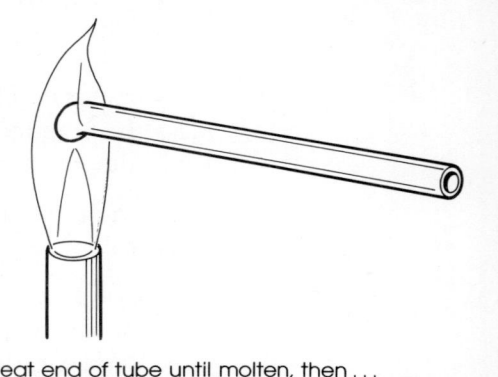

4 Heat end of tube until molten, then...

5 ...quickly blow the bulb a little out of the flame. Then repeat, heating the bulb until it collapses and blow again to twice the diameter of the tube.

CROSSWORD

First, trace the grid on to a piece of paper (or photocopy this page — teacher, please see the note at the front of the book). Then fill in the answers. Do not write on this book.

Across

2 Good area for a chemical factory (10)
8 Not a written exam (4)
9 A very important acid (6)
10 Ammonia has a distinctive ____ (5)
11 A farmer reaps as he ____ (4)
12 Pour this on troubled waters (3)
13 The process for manufacturing ammonia (5)
14 Worn before tights (6)
15 Solid fuel cooking range (3)
19 Modified cement (8)
22 Not a metric tonne (3)
23 The vapour can send you to sleep (5)
24 A useful alkaline gas (7)
27 Nickel (2)
28 A big word for soap-making (14)

Down

1 Sulphuric acid is made here (7)
2 Strong shiny substance (5)
3 Nothing succeeds like ____ (7)
4 Old name for sodium carbonate (4,3)

Down (*cont.*)

5 To give a thorough wetting (5)
6 A mistake in the experiment (5)
7 A big use for sodium carbonate (5)
16 Sulphuric in the rain? (4,4)
17 Shed a ____ for ammonia (4)
18 Famous sulphuric acid process (7)
19 A watery alternative to roads (6)
20 Fresh from Ordnance Survey (3,3)
21 Extraterrestrial being (2)
25 Huge chemical company (3)
26 Royal Institute of Chemistry (3)
27 Oxide of nitrogen (2)

EXERCISE

Write out the following sentences, filling in the blanks:

1 Fritz ____ was a German chemist who gave his name to the process to ____ ammonia from its elements ____ and ____.
   Ammonia can be converted into the important acid ____ ____ by mixing it with ____ and water. The catalyst is ____.
   Nitric acid can be used to make ____ for the farmer, ____ to brighten cloth and ____ for peaceful uses and ____.

2 _____ acid used to be considered as a _____ of prosperity _____ is now considered to be a more reliable _____ of economic _____.

3 Sodium chloride can be converted into the alkali _____ by the _____ of brine. The chlorine ion has a _____ charge and is therefore attracted to the _____ electrode. Valuable _____ gas is formed here. The sodium ion has a _____ charge and therefore goes to the _____ electrode. Sodium hydroxide can be used to make _____ compounds, _____ for wrapping and printing, _____ for wear and decoration and _____ for the washing process.

4 Cement is made by _____ a mixture of _____, _____ and _____ in a _____ kiln fired by ground _____. Some _____ is added to control setting _____. Concrete is cement plus _____, _____ and water. A new form of concrete may replace some _____ and _____ because of its reduced _____ size.

5 Glass is made from sodium carbonate, _____ and _____ when the mixture is heated to _____. Some _____ glass can be added as this saves on _____ and raw _____. It also keeps the _____ free of the _____ of discarded glass. _____ is used in glass-making to prevent the glass _____ in water.

6 If ammonia was spilled from a tanker my emergency _____ would be to notify _____ and fire-_____. I would _____ other road users and keep the _____ away from the _____ area. I would keep _____ wind to prevent suffocating and _____ protective _____ on entering the area.

CHAPTER 2

DRUGS AND DYES

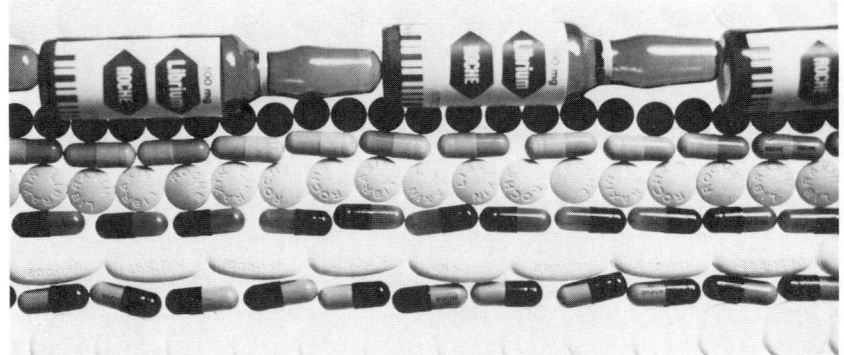

WHAT ARE DRUGS?

A drug is a chemical substance that can alter the processes of the body. The active ingredients of medicines are drugs. Even alcohol, nicotine and caffeine are drugs.

HOW DO DRUGS WORK?

Different drugs work in different ways but the action of most resembles that of one of the following four examples.

Opium

This drug has been used for over 6000 years. It has the power to relieve pain and to give a feeling of well-being. Opium is extracted from the opium poppy. It is now known that opium itself contains the powerful drugs morphine and codeine. Morphine is for the relief of intense pain, e.g. that of soldiers wounded in battle or of dying people. It is addictive and can only be given under a doctor's supervision. Codeine is a stronger painkiller than aspirin and is used in cough medicines and headache tablets.

Morphine can be changed into heroin, which is twice as good as a painkiller. Heroin is more addictive than morphine, and the medical profession rejects it as a painkiller for this reason. 'Drug-pushers' get their customers 'hooked' on heroin so that they will keep coming back to buy more.

Opium works as a drug because its molecule fits, like a key into a lock, into certain brain cells that are responsible for feeling pain. Many drugs work in this way.

Aspirin

The first relative of today's aspirin was isolated from the bark of the common white willow tree in the nineteenth century. The substance was called salicin after the Latin name for the tree. We swallow an average of 200 aspirins a year each in the UK. They are harmless as long as water is taken with them to reduce irritation of the stomach wall.

Aspirin relieves pain without being addictive. It also reduces swelling and fever by blocking an *enzyme* in the body. Enzymes are complicated molecules that control the chemical reactions in the body. When cells are injured an enzyme enables *prostaglandins* to be formed, and these cause swelling, fever and pain. Aspirin sticks to the *active site* of the enzyme (the part that causes the reaction), so that prostaglandins are no longer made, and the pain, swelling and fever subside. Many drugs are designed to attach themselves to the active sites of enzymes in this way.

Penicillin

Alexander Fleming discovered penicillin by chance in 1928. He had been growing bacteria on special culture plates. He noticed that one plate was contaminated with a mould. To his surprise the bacteria had stopped growing near the mould. The mould, *Penicillium notatum*, was killing the bacteria. Fleming showed that a substance from the mould, which he called *penicillin*, affected only certain types of bacteria. Some bacteria affected were the cause of human infection.

In 1945 the chemical structure of penicillin was discovered. This enabled chemists to make similar compounds that would attack even more harmful bacteria. Penicillin and its relatives are all examples of *antibiotic* drugs. Penicillins kill invading bacteria by attacking their cell walls just as they are about to divide into two bacteria. Their walls are weakened and they swell and burst. Human cells are quite different from those of bacteria and so are not damaged by penicillin.

Propranolol

Many drugs are designed for a particular task when the cause of the disease has been accurately pinpointed. Propranolol has been specially designed to prevent short bursts of chest pain known as *angina pectoris*. This pain is due to narrowing of the arteries supplying blood to the heart. The pain usually develops during exercise or severe emotional distress.

Nerves in the heart wall control its working. When these nerves are stimulated they release a substance called noradrenaline. Noradrenaline attaches itself to receptor cells, called *beta-receptors*, on the heart muscle, stimulating the heart to pump harder and faster. But the heart needs more oxygen from the blood to work harder. If the oxygen demand exceeds the supply the blood vessels narrow. The patient then suffers an attack of pain in the chest.

Sir James Black (1988 Nobel Prizewinner for Medicine) looked for a molecule that would occupy the beta-receptor sites without activating them to make noradrenaline. Such a drug would be a *beta-blocker*. The search led to the discovery of propranolol which is used widely to prevent angina.

Drugs such as cimetidine for stomach ulcers, salbutamol for asthma and allopurinol for gout, have all been designed to do their particular job after finding the cause of the illness.

The diagram on the next page shows the human body and the regions that certain drugs act upon to reduce suffering.

HOW ARE NEW DRUGS DEVELOPED?

The pharmaceutical companies can spend up to £100 million developing a new active ingredient. This can take them up to 12 years. It is a long and costly business and passes through various stages:

Research

1) Questions must be asked:

    - How many people suffer from the illness?
    - Are there alternative treatments available?
    - Can a profit be made?
    - Does the proposed drug fit in with our other drugs?
    - Do we have proper research facilities on site?

2) The search for a compound. It may take years to identify a likely drug. Compounds resembling natural ones in the body are tested. Also large numbers of different compounds may be extracted from plants or synthesised in the laboratory.

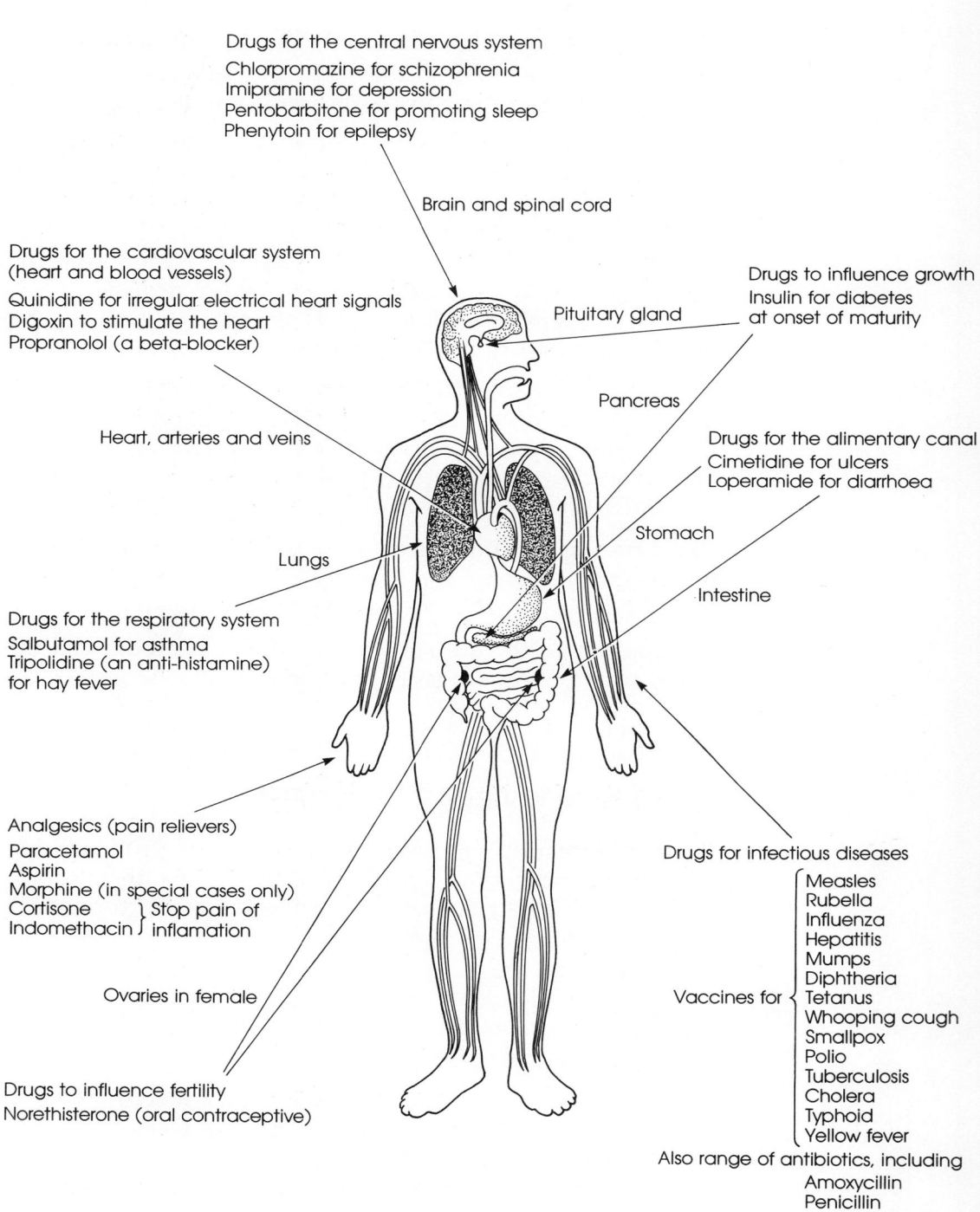

Some drugs and the regions on which they act

3) Research scientists test the drug. They will need to carry out experiments to answer these questions:
- Does the compound have the desired effect?
- Does the compound have any other beneficial effects?
- Are there any side-effects which are bad? If so, how serious are they?
- What happens to the drug in the body?

This research phase involves a great deal of testing on animals. In addition, estimates of the dose of the drug which would be fatal to humans must be made. Animal tests are strictly controlled by the Government in the UK, and are carried out to minimise the risk of harming humans.

If a drug looks promising it is patented by the pharmaceutical company. The patent lasts for 20 years and stops other companies from making the drug during this period without permission.

Development

Initial clinical trials. Provided that Government approval is given following a successful research phase, tests can then start on humans. This is the development phase. The first studies must be on VOLUNTEERS who have signed up with a full knowledge of what is going on. The volunteers are usually healthy and the test programme must be passed by an 'Ethics Committee'. This committee will be composed of local doctors, nurses, administrators and others. The scientists will want to know the answers to the following questions:
- How is the drug absorbed by the body?
- How is the drug distributed around the body?
- If the drug is broken down in the body, what substances are formed from it?
- Is the drug excreted from the body? If so, how long does it take to be completely removed?

Tests on human patients. It is not enough to know the drug's effect on healthy volunteers! Before it can be tested on patients, permission must be obtained from the Committee on Safety of Medicines. They study all results of earlier tests and decide whether it is safe to proceed.

In clinical tests on patients, some patients are given the drug and others are given a well-disguised 'dummy' substance, or *placebo*, which should have no effect on them. Then the two groups of patients are compared to make sure that any changes in their condition are actually due to the drug, rather than anything else. Any unwanted side-effects are also watched for.

Full clinical trials on patients. These can start only when a Clinical Trial Certificate has been awarded by the Committee on Safety of Medicines. These trials are carried out with large numbers of patients, and again placebos are used. Even the doctors conducting the trials must not know which medicine contains the drug! Afterwards, depending on the advice of the Committee on Safety of Medicines, the drug may then qualify for a Product Licence, and doctors can prescribe the drug to their patients.

Long-term clinical trials. These continue after the drug is on the market. Doctors are urged to report any harmful side-effects due to the drug.

The graph below shows the general changes in cash flow for making a new successful drug. Study the curve and answer the questions:

1) Roughly at which year is the investment the greatest?

2) How many years have passed before the launch of the drug in the UK and the USA?

3) How many years into the project does the drug start to make money?

4) Why do the profits start to slow down when the patent expires?

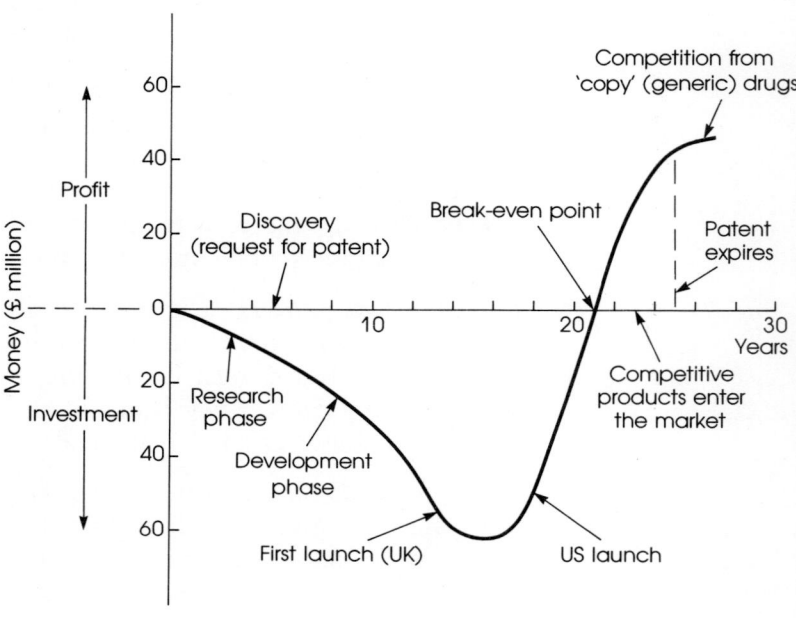

A typical cash flow curve for making a drug

THE TOP TEN DRUGS IN THE WORLD

The table below shows the top ten drugs by sales value worldwide for the year 1982:

Brand name	Chemical name	Manufacturer	What it does
Tagamet	Cimetidine	Smith, Kline & French	Helps to heal ulcers
Keflex	Cephalexin	Lilly	Antibiotic
Inderal	Propranolol	ICI	Beta-blocker
Aldomet	Alpha-methyldopa	Merck, Sharpe & Dohme	Lowers blood pressure
Naprosyn	Naproxen	Syntex	Relieves pain of arthritis
Brufen	Ibuprofen	Boots	Relieves pain of arthritis
Valium	Diazepam	Roche	Reduces nervous anxiety
Feldene	Piroxicam	Pfizer	Relieves pain of arthritis
Adalat	Nifedipine	Bayer	Reduces heart attacks
Septrin	Sulphamethoxazole	Wellcome	Antibiotic

Answer these questions on the table:

1) How many of the top drugs are involved in the treatment of (a) arthritis, (b) the heart, (c) bacterial infection?

2) What is a beta-blocker? How does it work?

3) Are there any obvious UK manufacturers in this list? If so, name them.

OPREN

In spite of the thorough testing that drugs undergo before they are released on the market, mistakes are still made. Opren was a drug manufactured by Eli Lilly to help sufferers of arthritis. Over the years that it was on the market it must have relieved a great deal of suffering, but in 1982 it was withdrawn because it had been linked with 74 deaths and 4000 cases of illness. It was claimed that the drug caused kidney and liver failure, skin diseases and acute sensitivity to light.

In December 1987, 1350 UK victims of the drug were offered compensation by the manufacturer, but this amounted to an average of less than £2000 each. Also a condition of accepting the offer was that the victims dropped any further legal claims against the drug, and no compensation would be forthcoming unless the majority did accept.

The legal costs that could be incurred by pressing for more realistic compensation leave these people little option but to accept the offer, but it has been proposed that Legal Aid should be available in future for fighting cases of this kind. MPs have also suggested setting up a trust fund to help the victims, and there is even talk of boycotting Eli Lilly products unless better terms are agreed to.

THE MANUFACTURE OF PENICILLIN

Most drugs are manufactured from chemicals in a long series of reactions, but some, such as penicillin, are made by organisms and then extracted. The stages in the manufacture of penicillin from the mould *Penicillium chrysogenum* are as follows:

1) The spores of the mould are encouraged to grow in a medium such as malt extract.

2) The growing organism is added to a fermenter which may hold as much as 200 cubic metres. Here it is mixed with water at a strictly controlled temperature. The organism is provided with its *substrate*, the chemicals that it needs to feed on. These may include carbohydrates, phosphates, ammonia, oxygen and organic acids. Under strict conditions the organism makes only one penicillin. Different strains of the organism are used to make different penicillins.

3) The fermentation mixture is filtered and penicillin is extracted from the filtrate.

Up to 70 g of penicillin can be made by feeding the organism with one kilogram of carbohydrate. Some 20 000 tonnes of penicillin are made worldwide each year. The cost is only about £16 per kilogram by this biochemical fermentation process. The cost would be much higher if penicillin were produced by purely chemical processes. The natural penicillins are useful antibiotics. The cultured penicillins are even better because they can attack a wider range of bacteria.

For more information on penicillin and other antibiotics see Extending Science 11: *Biotechnology* by J Teasdale (ST(P)).

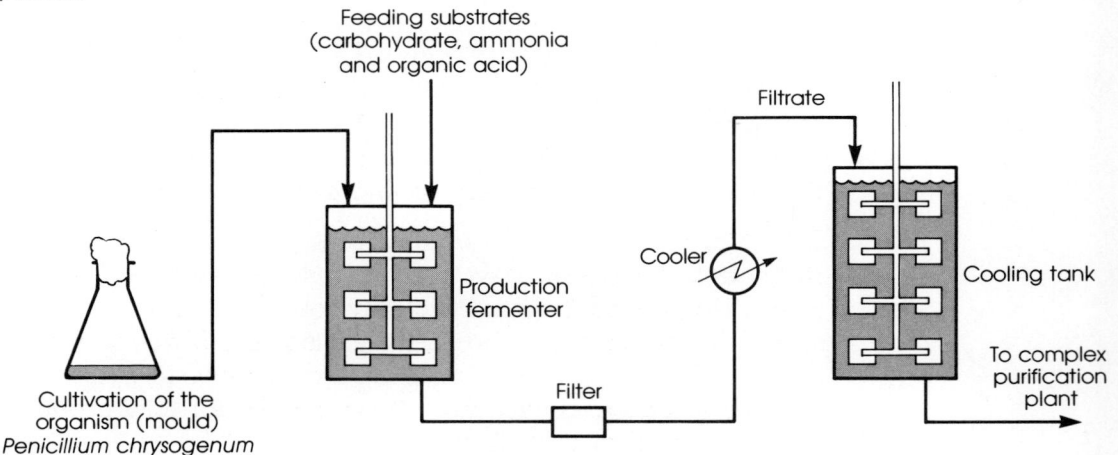

The manufacture of penicillin

ACTIVITY 4	**To show antibiotic nature (antibiosis)**

1) Add nutrient agar (low concentration) to a petri dish.

2) Add a little garden or field soil evenly to the petri dish and place the lid on it. Leave at room temperature for up to ten days.

3) Look at the dish every day. You should see colonies of soil bacteria growing on the agar. As they become crowded some bacteria will produce poisonous, antibiotic substances. The presence of the poisons will be shown by clear zones around some colonies of bacteria.

DYES

The UK produces over 50 000 tonnes of dyes worth £200 million each year. The UK is the fourth biggest producer of dyes in the world. Only Germany, the USA and Japan exceed the UK production.

Dyes are usually organic in nature, i.e. they are compounds of carbon and hydrogen and sometimes oxygen, nitrogen and sulphur. The coloured substances in animals and plants are dyes.

Inorganic dyes are found in ceramics, enamels, glasses and some rocks.

Physical dyes are not really dyes at all; they are things that look coloured because they split up the light much as a glass prism does. Examples of physical dyes are coloured insect wings, birds' feathers, a blue sky and sunset.

W H Perkin in 1856 was the first person to make a dye. He made it by accident and it was called mauveine. This was a very popular colour in Victorian ladies' wear. The dye was based on the tar obtained by heating coal out of contact with air. Most of the dyes made today are still based on chemicals obtained from coal tar.

There is such a wide variety of fabrics that thousands of dyes are now required. Good dyes possess the following qualities:

- An intense colour.
- They usually dissolve in water.
- They are absorbed by, or react with, the fibres of the fabric.
- They should survive manufacture and use, i.e. they should be fast.

There are over twelve general types of which the six most common are as follows:

Type of dye	Description
Acid	Negatively charged, applied from an acid dye bath.
Mordant	A chemical is used to bind the dye to the fabric.
Basic	Positively charged, applied from an alkaline dyebath.
Disperse	Hardly soluble in water, simply very fine particles in suspension.
Azoic	Two solutions are mixed on cloth to form an insoluble dye.
Reactive	It actually forms strong chemical bonds with the fabric.

Which dyes for which cloth?

Rotary screen printing of furnishing fabric

The table shows how different dyes can be used for different fibres. CA stands for cellulose acetates, PA for polyamide, PES for polyester and PAC for polyacrylonitrile. $\checkmark$ = dye suitable for this fabric.

Type of dye	Wool	Cotton	CA	PA	PES	PAC
Acid	✓			✓		
Mordant	✓			✓		
Basic	✓	✓	✓	✓	✓	✓
Disperse			✓	✓	✓	✓
Azoic		✓	✓		✓	
Reactive	✓	✓				

Use the table to answer these questions:

1) Which dyes would you never use to colour wool?
2) Which dye would be a safe bet even if the type of cloth was unknown?
3) The use of synthetic fibres — polyamide, polyester and polyacrylonitrile — is increasing dramatically in the world. Other fibres are on the decrease. Which dyes are going to be most useful in the future?

THE MANUFACTURE OF A DYE

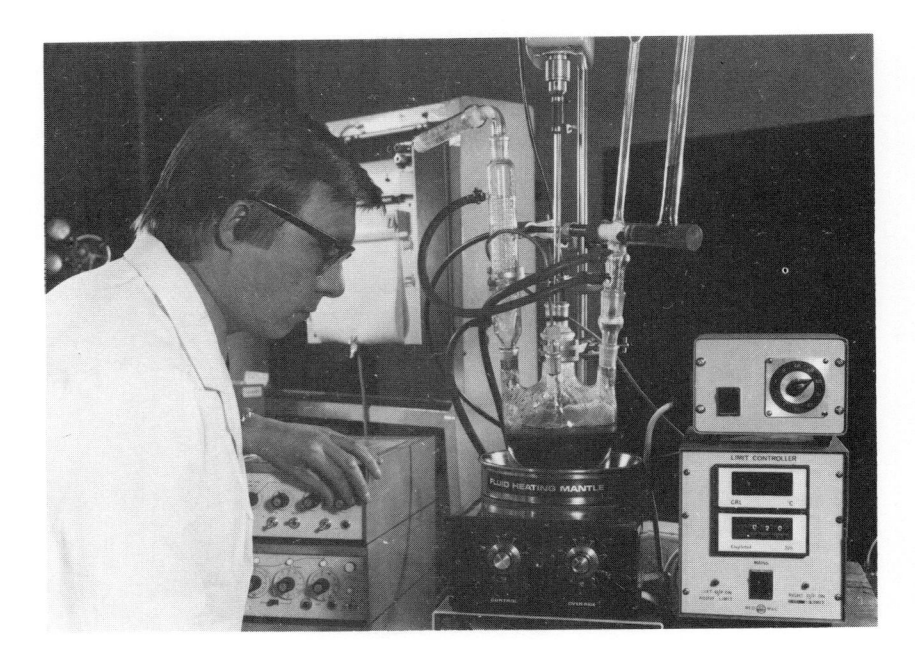

Automated control of the laboratory-scale preparation of a dye

Sudan Orange is a dye used to colour waxes in candles, shoe and floor polishes. It is also used for coloured smoke and polystyrene resins. The stages of its manufacture are shown in the flow diagram on the next page.

ACTIVITY 5

Making Sudan Orange on a small scale

Wear plastic or rubber gloves for this experiment.

1) Add 5 drops of phenylamine to a boiling-tube using a teat pipette. Phenylamine MUST NOT touch the skin. Add 30 drops of dilute hydrochloric acid to the phenylamine and mix with a glass rod. Surround the boiling-tube with a mixture of ice, water and common salt in a beaker.

2) Dissolve about one gram of sodium nitrite in as little distilled water as possible in a boiling-tube. Cool this solution in the beaker also.

3) After about ten minutes of cooling the solutions, add the sodium nitrite solution to the phenylamine solution. Continue to cool the mixture.

4) Dissolve just a few crystals of beta-naphthol in ten drops of dilute sodium hydroxide in another boiling-tube. Stir with a clean glass rod.

5) Add the solution from 4) to the solution from 3). Note the bright orange dye formed and then pour some on to cotton cloth.

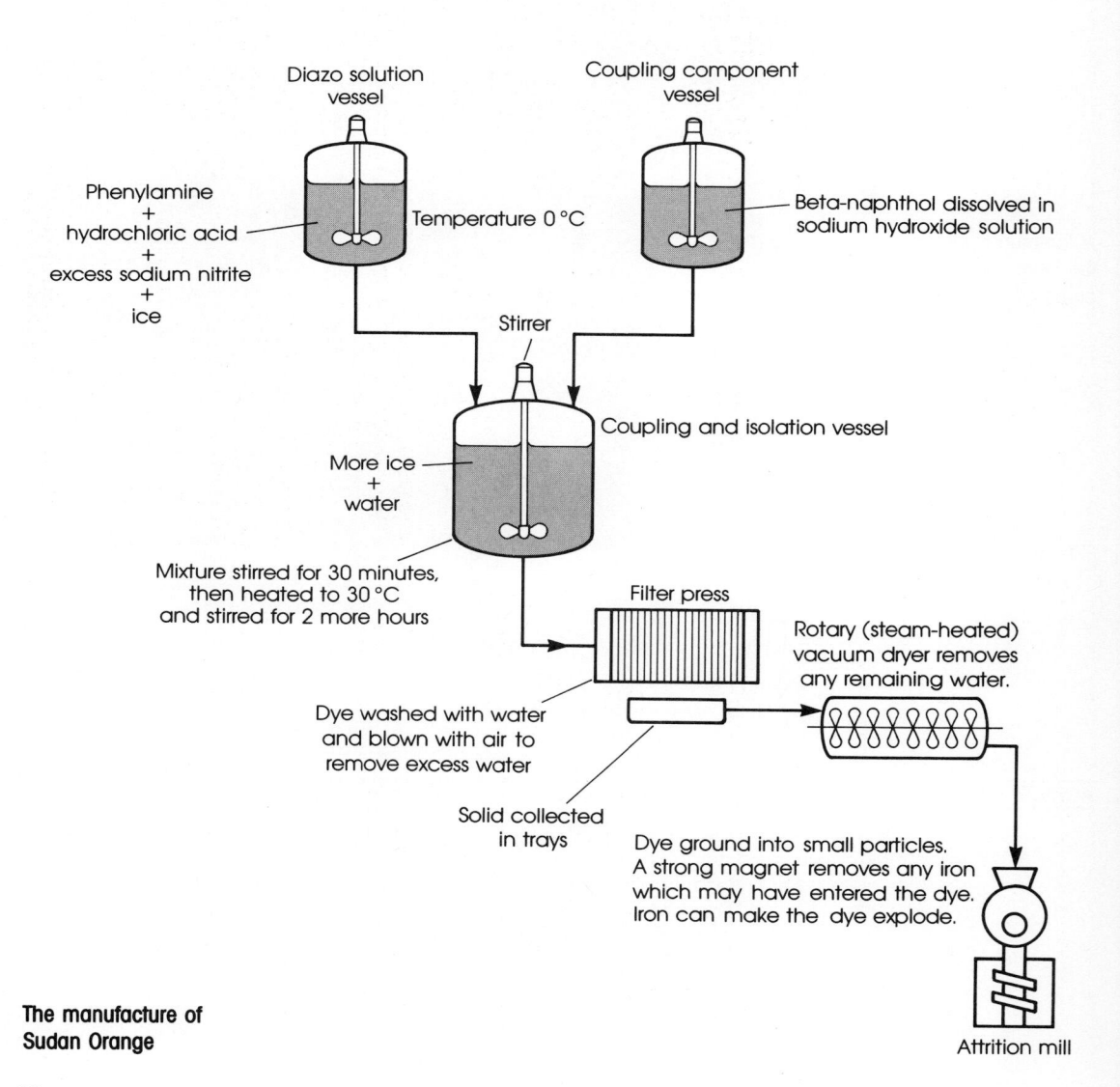

The manufacture of Sudan Orange

Diazo solution vessel — Phenylamine + hydrochloric acid + excess sodium nitrite + ice — Temperature 0 °C

Coupling component vessel — Beta-naphthol dissolved in sodium hydroxide solution

Coupling and isolation vessel — Stirrer — More ice + water

Mixture stirred for 30 minutes, then heated to 30 °C and stirred for 2 more hours

Filter press — Dye washed with water and blown with air to remove excess water — Solid collected in trays

Rotary (steam-heated) vacuum dryer removes any remaining water.

Dye ground into small particles. A strong magnet removes any iron which may have entered the dye. Iron can make the dye explode.

Attrition mill

EXERCISE

Rewrite the following sentences, filling in the blanks:

1 Some drugs like _____ have been in use for over 6000 _____. Many drugs work like a _____ in a lock; they often _____ the lock, thus minimising the _____. Aspirin derives from a drug extracted from the white _____ _____. It relieves _____ as well as swelling and _____.

2 _____ was discovered in a _____ by Alexander _____. Today many such _____ are prepared to cover the many different _____ that attack us.

3 Making a drug can take up to _____ years. Drugs like _____ have made people suspicious of the _____ - _____ of these chemicals. It is a _____ time before _____ companies regain their _____, let alone a profit. When the _____ expires other companies can _____ the drug without _____. This also cuts down on company _____ but is good for the _____.

4 Propranolol is a _____-_____. It stops _____ being secreted from the _____ cells. Thus the _____ does not race, requiring too much _____ to work. This drug prevents _____, which is a disease of the _____ involving _____ of the arteries, and _____.

5 Analgesics relieve _____ whilst norethisterone prevents unwanted _____. _____ fight bacteria that would cause _____ in _____. The top selling drug in the world is surprisingly one for _____. It is called _____ and is made by _____.

CHAPTER 3
LIQUID GOLD — TO THE CHEMIST

Few could guess the treasures within the black smelly liquid that is crude oil. It fuels our travels over land, sea and air. It powers much of our industry by generating electricity. It lubricates the world's machinery and surfaces our roads. A wealth of new chemicals are made from this uninviting liquid.

Nobody knows for certain how the oil was first formed. A popular theory is that it comes from animals and plants which lived in the sea. Millions of years of pressure and high temperature have converted them into oil and gas.

There are four main oil-producing areas of the world: the USA, the Middle East, Caribbean countries and the USSR.

Prospecting for new oil deposits has been successful in the continental shelf areas at sea; witness the North Sea deposits off the United Kingdom. Inland areas showing promise are those with sedimentary rock deposits. There is also great interest in the untapped mineral wealth of Alaska, which includes oil.

HOW DO THEY FIND THE OIL?

No one can say for certain where crude oil lies. A mixture of intelligent detective work and expensive drilling is the best route. The computer has made things much easier. Whether oil is suspected on land or at sea, a seismic survey must first be made. This seismic survey involves the stages shown on the next page.

Such a survey can penetrate thousands of feet below the sea bed or earth's surface. The data collected are stored on a computer, then transmitted to the main processing centre. Experts in rock formations, geophysicists, observe the computer pictures. They can print out sections of the rock structure which seem of interest. The experts on the oil in such a structure are called reservoir engineers. They decide how best to produce oil from the reservoir.

Detectors to collect reflected sound waves

Compressed-air gun (sends out the signal)

SEISMIC SURVEY

Data sent onshore to computers

Data processed by computer

Print out

Three-dimensional picture of the oil well

Under 'normal' light

Using fluorescent photography

CORE SAMPLES

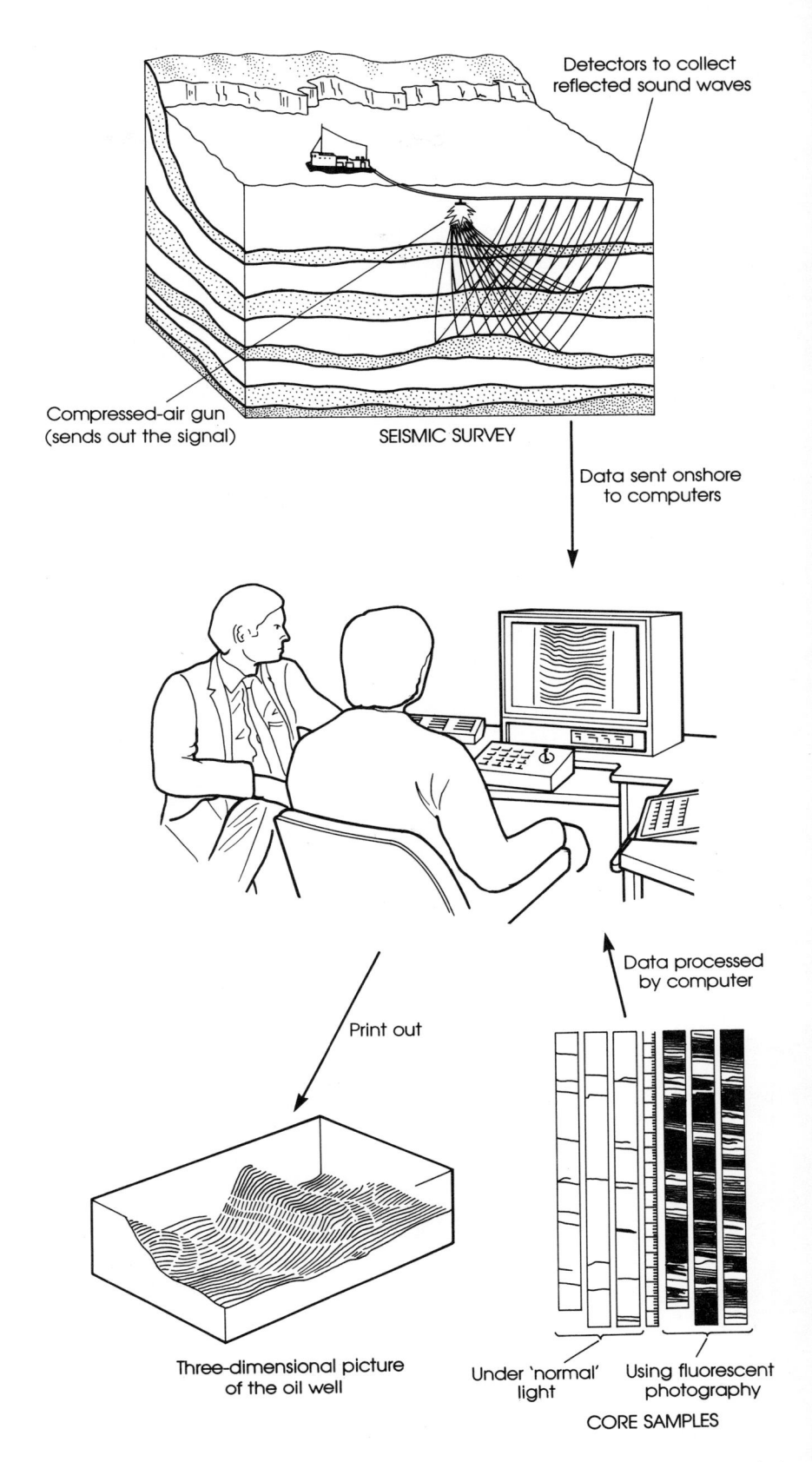

Where is the oil?

41

HOW DO THEY GET THE OIL OUT?

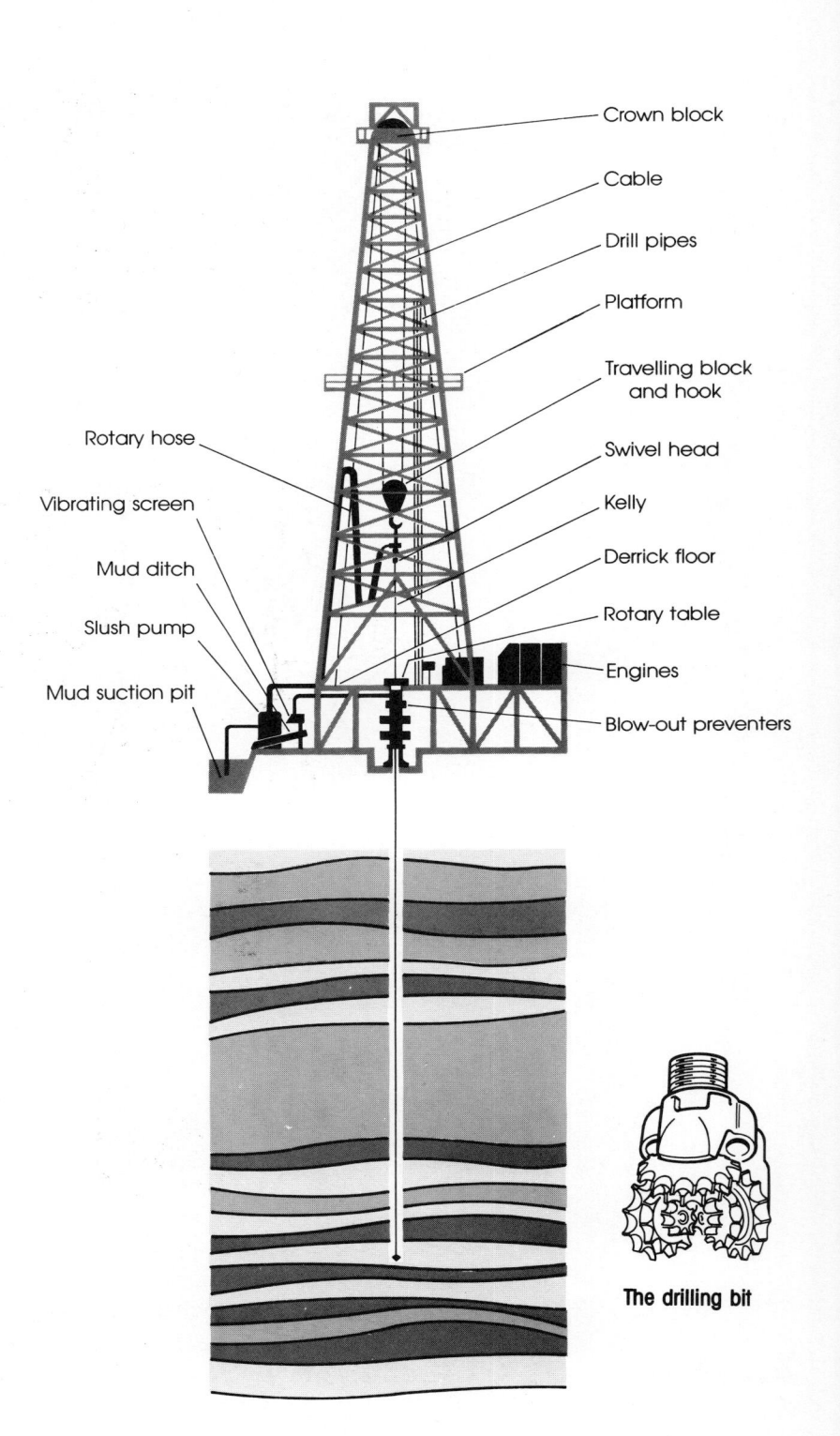

- Crown block
- Cable
- Drill pipes
- Platform
- Travelling block and hook
- Rotary hose
- Vibrating screen
- Swivel head
- Kelly
- Mud ditch
- Derrick floor
- Slush pump
- Rotary table
- Engines
- Mud suction pit
- Blow-out preventers

The drilling bit

An oil well

Finding the oil is difficult enough; bringing it to the surface is even more of a challenge. The offshore drilling platform can operate up to 30 different wells. Different angles are used to reach the best parts of the reservoir. Platform positions and the best direction for each well are calculated by computer. Core samples help to pinpoint ideal routes. Over the lifetime of a large oilfield hundreds of wells may be drilled. Each drilling can cost several million pounds. It is important to drill in the right place!

The drill is made of specially tough metal and usually diamond teeth are used. These teeth must be able to cut through the hardest rock. The drill is rotated as it burrows below the surface. The drilling bit is driven by a square hollow pipe called the *kelly*. This kelly passes through a square hole in a rotating table. The table is turned by diesel power. the kelly turns with it, twisting the drilling bit into the ground. The drill goes deeper and runs out of pipe. It is stopped and another 9 metre section of drill pipe is screwed in.

The drill would soon overheat without a cooling system. Mud — a mixture of clay, some chemicals and water — is used as the coolant. It is constantly pumped down the drill pipe and comes out through holes in the bit. The mud returns to the surface with drill fragments, which are examined, both for oil and to see which type of rock is present. The mud also controls the escape of gas or oil, preventing a blow-out. Sometimes drilling can be as fast as 60 metres an hour, but in particularly hard rock can be as slow as 30 centimetres an hour! The depth of most wells is between 900 and 5000 metres. No wonder it is such an expensive process!

When the well is into production the drilling rig is taken away. It is replaced by an assembly of pipes known as a 'Christmas tree'. These pipes seal the well-head and control the flow of oil. In the past, wells were often abandoned when only 20 per cent of the oil had been recovered. Now, water or gas is injected into the oil reservoir. This increases the pressure and forces up to 40 per cent of the oil out of the porous rock.

World oil production

The graph of world oil production on the next page shows huge increases over the years. The demand may well have fallen since 1980 because of its high price compared with that of other fuels. Many countries have been short of funds to buy oil in the 1980s and have needed to reduce their consumption of it.

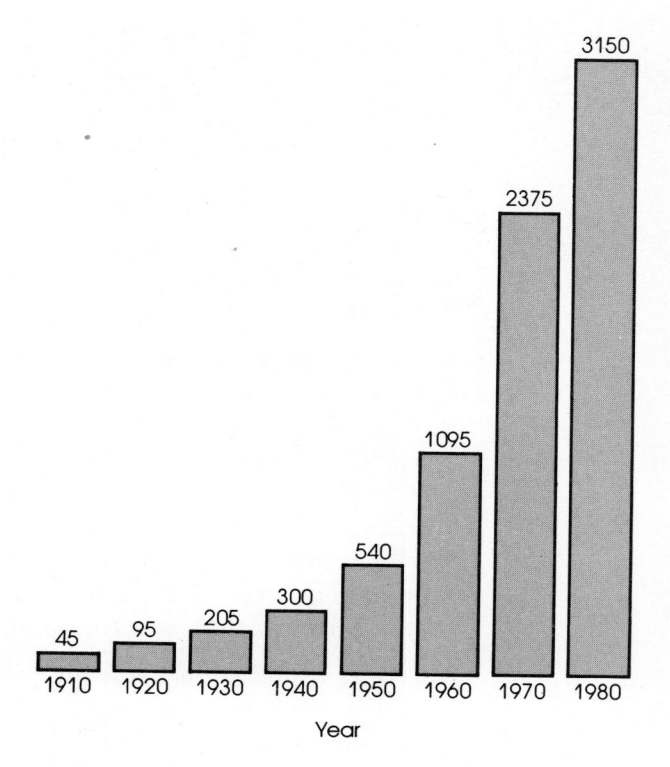

World crude oil production (millions of tonnes)

Year	Production
1910	45
1920	95
1930	205
1940	300
1950	540
1960	1095
1970	2375
1980	3150

NORTH SEA OIL AND GAS FIELDS

Look at the map showing the oil and gas fields around the UK. The huge area surrounding the UK map represents UK waters. Use the map to answer the following questions:

1) Calculate the total number of (a) oilfields, (b) gas fields.

2) Name the oilfields that have more than 230 million tonnes of oil.

3) Name the oilfields that have less than 30 million tonnes of oil.

4) Name the gas fields that contain between 84 and 127 billion cubic metres of gas.

5) Use the map scale to estimate the lengths of the pipelines to the mainland from (a) Ekofisk, (b) Forbes, (c) Frigg, (d) Brae.

6) Estimate the total oil (in millions of tonnes) present in the North Sea oil fields.

7) Name two fields outside UK waters, but on the map.

North Sea oil and gas fields

Inset (northern area):
- MAGNUS
- THISTLE
- DEVERON
- MURCHISON
- N CORMORANT
- DUNLIN
- NW HUTTON
- STATFJORD (UK)
- S CORMORANT
- BRENT
- HUTTON
- HEATHER
- NINIAN
- ALWYN NORTH

Main map labels:
- Sullom Voe
- Shetland Islands
- FRIGG
- BERYL
- Orkney Islands
- "FLAGS" line
- N & S BRAE
- Flotta
- PIPER
- BALMORAL
- CLAYMORE
- TARTAN
- CYRUS
- HIGHLANDER
- MAUREEN
- BEATRICE
- Nigg Bay
- BUCHAN
- FORTIES
- St Fergus
- MONTROSE
- Cruden Bay
- FULMAR
- CLYDE
- AUK
- EKOFISK
- INNES
- ARGYLL
- DUNCAN
- FORBES
- Teesside
- ESMOND
- GORDON
- ROUGH
- WEST SOLE
- VIKING
- S. MORECAMBE
- VICTOR
- Easington
- INDEFATIGABLE
- Theddlethorpe
- SEAN
- HEWETT
- LEMAN
- Bacton

Legend:
- —— OIL PIPELINE(S)
- ---- GAS PIPELINE(S)
- ○ TERMINAL

OIL FIELD Million tonnes
- · UNDER 30
- ● 38–75
- ● 106–143
- ● 230 AND OVER

GAS FIELD Billion cubic metres
- ▪ UNDER 20
- ■ 48
- ■ 84–127
- ■ 298

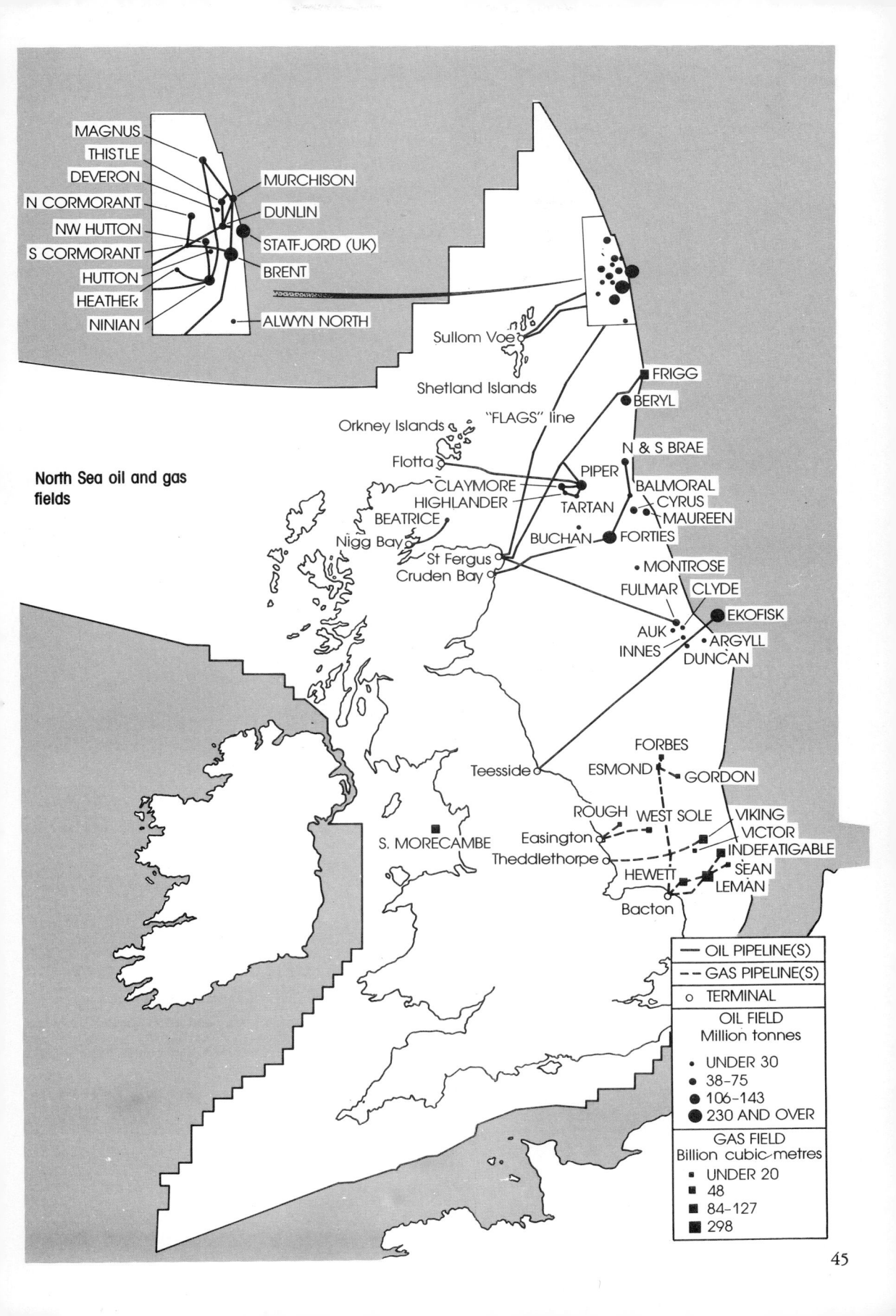

WHAT DOES CRUDE OIL CONTAIN?

Crude oil is a mixture of hundreds of different chemicals. The chemicals have one similarity in that they are all *hydrocarbons* (except for traces of compounds containing sulphur, chlorine or oxygen). Hydrocarbons are made up of the elements hydrogen and carbon only. Look at the structures of some of the hydrocarbons found in crude oil and answer the questions:

1) Count the number of carbon atoms and hydrogen atoms in each molecule and then write down the *formula* of each, e.g. molecule (a) has 2C's and 6H's, giving a formula of C_2H_6.

2) Count the number of bonds (lines) coming out from each carbon atom. Does the number of bonds ever vary in the examples?

3) Molecules (a), (b), (d), (f), (g), (i), (k) and (l) are all members of one series of hydrocarbons called *alkanes* (once called paraffins). Can you find the similarities between them by looking at their structures and their formulae?

4) Look at molecules (c) and (j). They are from a series of compounds called *cycloalkanes* also found in crude oil. What is similar about their structures?

5) Look at molecules (e) and (h). Can you see a similarity in their structures? These two are called *aromatic* hydrocarbons.

6) Look at molecule (l). Can you see one way in which its structure is different from the other alkanes considered in question 3)?

There are lots of molecules in crude oil other than those shown. Most of them are alkanes, but several of them are cycloalkanes and aromatic hydrocarbons.

Natural gas is always found with crude oil. In fact crude oil contains natural gas dissolved in it. Write a list of the formulae of the alkanes (d), (a), (i) and (b). Their names in this order are *methane, ethane, propane* and *butane*, the four main gases in natural gas. Natural gas is often said to be simply methane because this is present in the biggest percentage.

Crude oil can vary from place to place. Oil from Kuwait will be different from North Sea oil. The differences are only slight, however, and all oil contains mainly alkanes, with some aromatic hydrocarbons and cycloalkanes. Most crude oils contain molecules having up to 40 carbon atoms, i.e. roughly twice as many as in molecule (g)!

SEPARATING OIL INTO ITS USEFUL PARTS

Crude oil, as taken out of the ground, is not useful at all. It must be separated into its useful parts (*fractions*) by *fractional distillation*. Also some fractions are improved for use by breaking up the molecules, these broken molecules regrouping

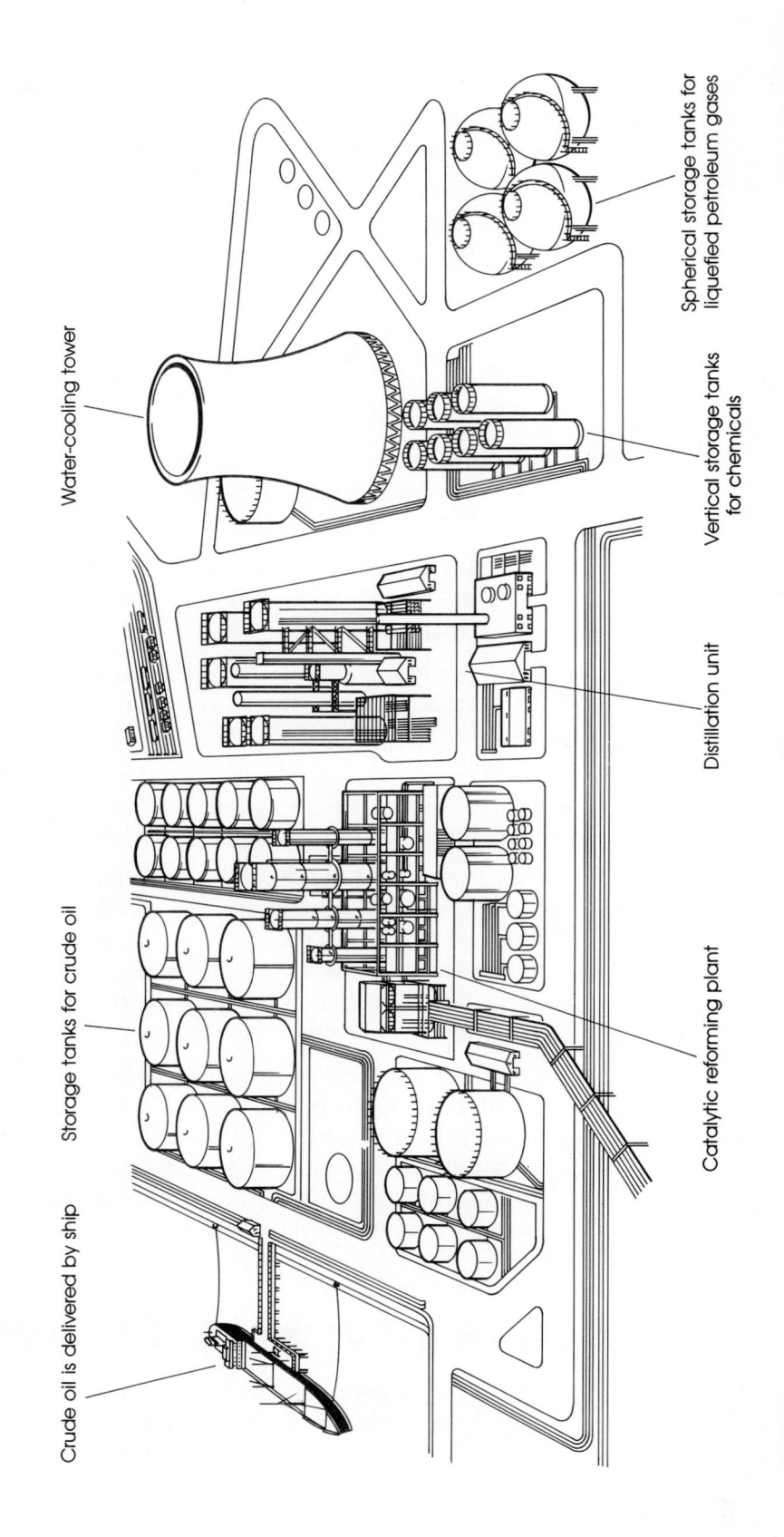

Spherical storage tanks for liquefied petroleum gases

Water-cooling tower

Vertical storage tanks for chemicals

Distillation unit

Catalytic reforming plant

Storage tanks for crude oil

Crude oil is delivered by ship

An oil refinery

to make new hydrocarbons. These breaking processes are called *cracking* and *reforming*. The place where fractional distillation, cracking and reforming are done is called an *oil refinery*.

Look at the picture of a typical oil refinery. The crude oil will be delivered to it by tanker, so the refinery will be very close to a deep-sea port. A system of pipes takes the stored crude oil to the various parts of the chemical plant. Fractional distillation is the first priority, then suitable fractions can be cracked or reformed. The gases given off are stored, as liquids, under high pressure in the spherical tanks. The useful products of the refinery will be sold off to travel by road, rail or sea.

FRACTIONAL DISTILLATION

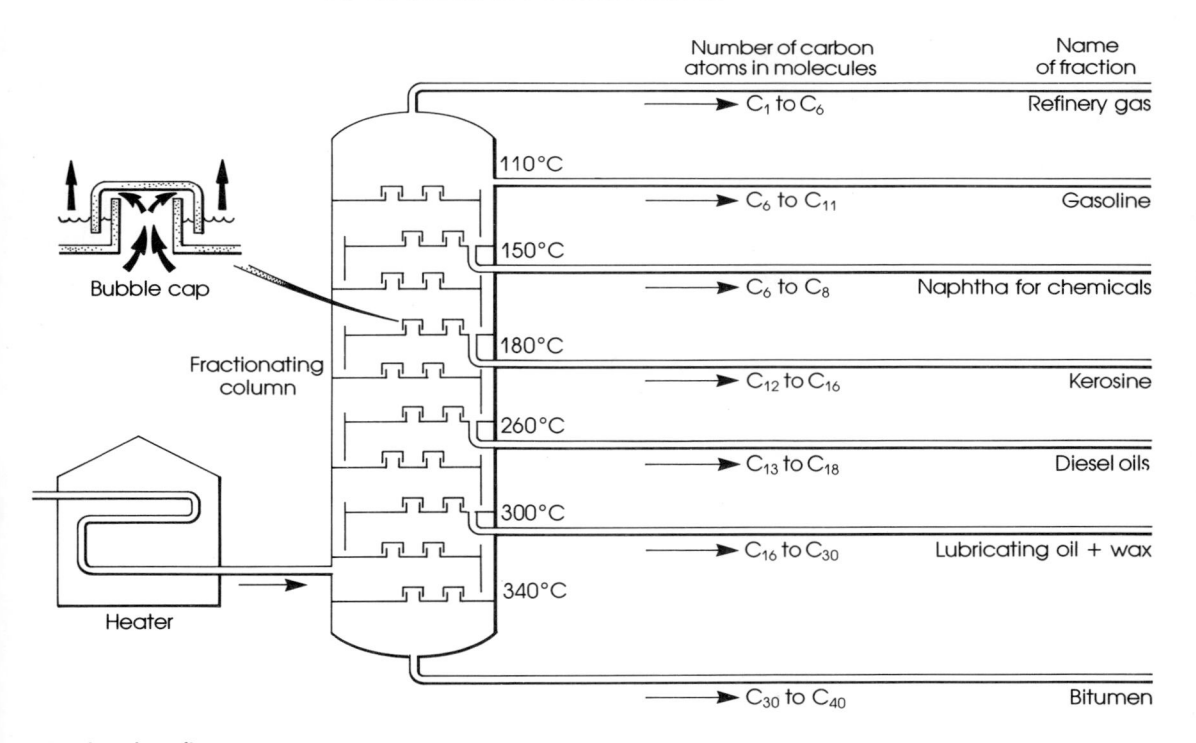

Temperature	Number of carbon atoms in molecules	Name of fraction
	C_1 to C_6	Refinery gas
110°C	C_6 to C_{11}	Gasoline
150°C	C_6 to C_8	Naphtha for chemicals
180°C	C_{12} to C_{16}	Kerosine
260°C	C_{13} to C_{18}	Diesel oils
300°C	C_{16} to C_{30}	Lubricating oil + wax
340°C		
	C_{30} to C_{40}	Bitumen

Fractionating oil

Look at the diagram above. The stages of fractional distillation are:

1) Crude oil is heated in a furnace to about 400 °C.

2) The oil vapour goes into the tall steel tower known as a *fractionating column*.

3) You will see that there are many trays with holes in them. There is a dome over each hole making a bubble cap. The hot vapour rises through the bubble cap. Some of the hot vapour condenses to form a liquid on the tray. Other parts of the vapour go higher to the next tray, and so on.

4) The temperature gets lower as the vapour goes up the column. Thus the vapour separates because different components have differing boiling points, and therefore condense at different temperatures.

In this way the smelly, black, crude oil is separated into fractions with wonderful uses. The smallest molecules, containing one to six carbon atoms, come in the top fraction at the lowest temperature. The largest molecules, with thirty to forty carbon atoms, come in the lowest fraction at the highest temperature.

CRACKING

The most useful fractions of crude oil are the lighter ones, and so there is a great demand for these. Over half of the fractions obtained from crude oil, however, are the heavier, less useful ones. Cracking offers the chance of breaking the less useful bigger molecules into useful smaller ones. The flow diagram shows the stages in the cracking process.

The cracking process always involves:

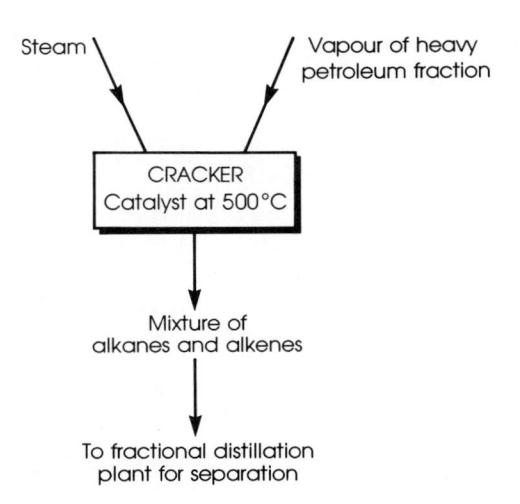

```
       Steam \           / Vapour of heavy
              \         /  petroleum fraction
               \       /
              ┌─────────┐
              │ CRACKER │
              │Catalyst │
              │at 500°C │
              └─────────┘
                   │
                   ▼
            Mixture of
         alkanes and alkenes
                   │
                   ▼
         To fractional distillation
          plant for separation
```

The cracking process

Larger alkane → Alkene + Smaller alkane

e.g. C_6H_{14} → C_2H_4 + C_4H_{10}
       Hexane → Ethene + Butane

| ACTIVITY 6 | **Cracking medical paraffin** |

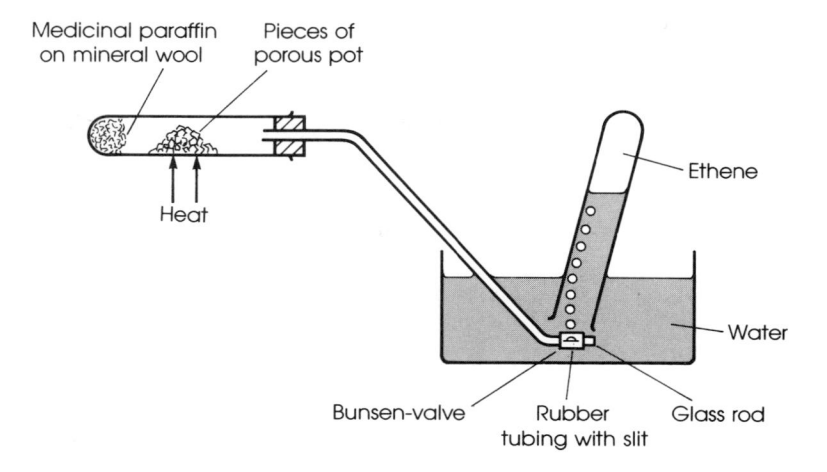

1) Add ten drops of medicinal paraffin to some mineral wool at the end of a pyrex boiling tube.

2) Set up the apparatus as shown, making sure to have a Bunsen valve to prevent suck-back of water.

3) Heat the porous porcelain pot. From time to time, warm the mineral wool. Collect the gas given off over water in test-tubes.

4) Test the gas for (a) smell, (b) ability to burn when touched with a lighted splint, (c) its effect when shaken with a few drops of bromine water.

REFORMING

This process is similar to cracking in that it involves breaking molecules. Once again a catalyst and pressure are required, but this time the molecules are usually cycloalkanes rather than alkanes. The cycloalkanes break and *reform* into aromatic hydrocarbons. This process particularly helps in making petrol for cars.

OTHER SUBSTANCES FROM OIL

Some of the chemicals in the oil fractions are very reactive. They combine with each other or with chemicals from elsewhere. They can be used to make complicated substances of great value. For example, benzene, acetone (also called propanone) and alcohols can be made from oil fractions. These dissolve many substances and are therefore widely used as solvents. Such solvents used to be made by more complicated routes from coal and sugar-beet. Also, the cheapest way to make nitrogen-containing fertilisers now is from natural gas. The diagram below shows some of the uses of chemicals from crude oil.

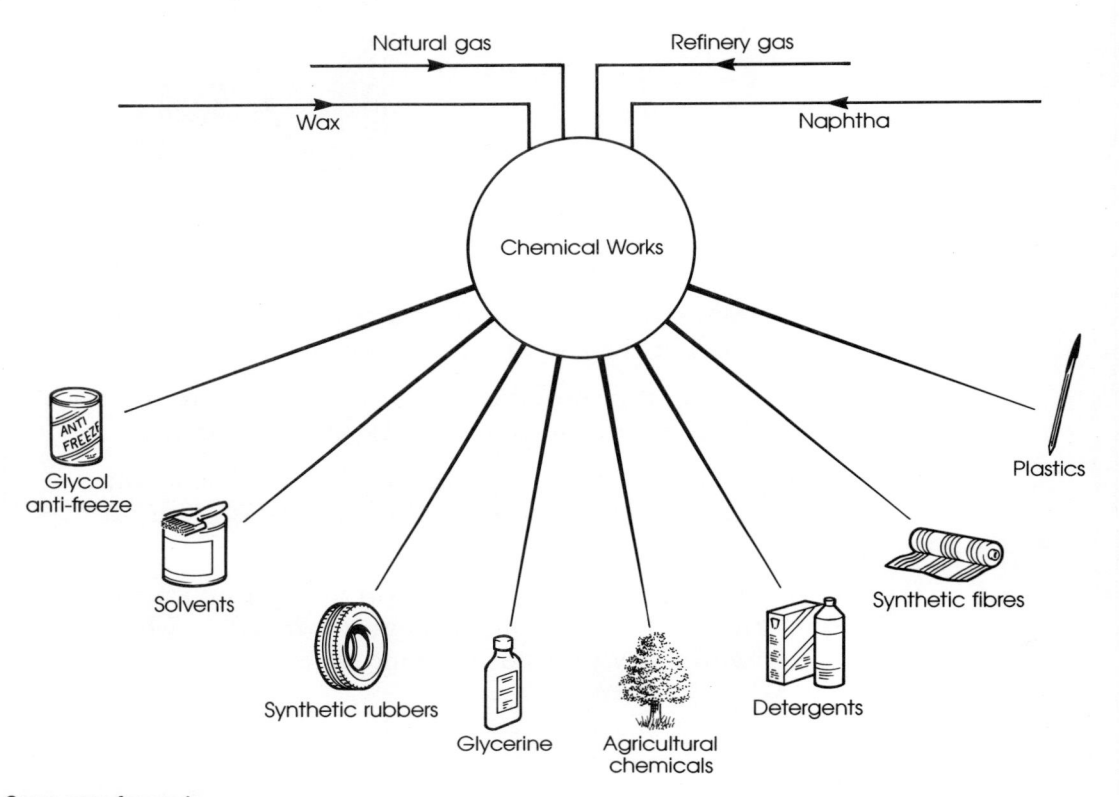

Some uses for crude oil chemicals

ACTIVITY 7

Making a soapless detergent

1) Place 1 cm^3 of castor oil in a Pyrex boiling-tube. Place the boiling tube in a rack.

2) Your teacher will add concentrated sulphuric acid drop by drop to the castor oil. Stir the mixture with a glass rod after each addition of acid. You MUST wear safety goggles. The stirrer must NOT be taken out and rested on the bench. Great CARE is required when handling this acid.

3) Stir the mixture with a glass rod for a few minutes to mix it thoroughly. Is there a change in temperature?

4) Pour the oily contents into a test-tube containing about 5 cm³ of water. Stir the mixture and pour off the liquid into the sink. This is the washing procedure to remove any remaining acid. Repeat the washing.

5) The solid is a detergent. Try it out by shaking with water to give foam.

HOW DOES THE WORLD USE OIL?

The two pie charts below show various uses of oil in the world (excluding Communist countries) by percentage for the year 1982. It also predicts what the percentage will be in the year 2000. The size of the circles are meant to give an impression of the relative quantities of oil used (or to be used).

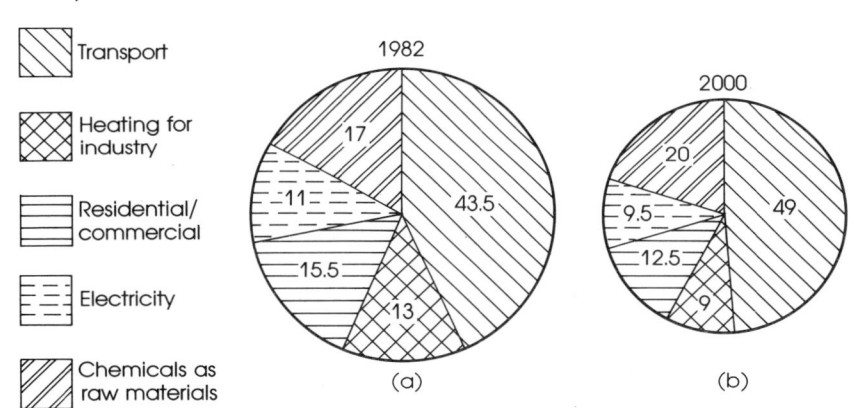

Uses of crude oil in (a) 1982, (b) 2000

Key:
- Transport
- Heating for industry
- Residential/commercial
- Electricity
- Chemicals as raw materials

1982: Transport 43.5, Heating for industry 13, Residential/commercial 15.5, Electricity 11, Chemicals as raw materials 17

2000: Transport 49, Heating for industry 9, Residential/commercial 12.5, Electricity 9.5, Chemicals as raw materials 20

Answer the following questions from the pie charts:

1) List the many uses for oil in each of the categories: transport (fuel to power lorries, cars, boats, trains, aeroplanes, etc.) heating for industry, residential/commercial (heating for houses and shops), electricity (generated from the heat of burning oil) and chemicals to make plastics, detergents, fibres, agricultural chemicals, solvents, etc. (but not to provide energy).

2) What was the chief use of oil in 1982?

3) What was the second largest use for oil in 1982?

4) The circle for year 2000 is smaller. Why do you think the consumption of oil is expected to decrease?

5) Which uses form a greater percentage of the total consumption in 2000 than they did in 1982? What do you think is the reason for this?

6) Which uses form a smaller percentage of the total in 2000 than in 1982? What do you think is the reason for the difference?

ALCOHOL TO REPLACE OIL IN THE NEXT CENTURY?

Oil, as we have seen, is the raw material from which many chemicals are made. If the supply of oil runs out, therefore, alternatives must be found. The alcohol *ethanol* could be the answer to the problem.

Besides being the alcohol in alcoholic drinks, ethanol has many industrial uses. It is used as a solvent and is used in the manufacture of other chemicals. In the future it could be used to make some of the chemicals that are now made from oil. For example, it can easily be converted into ethene, the basis of many plastics.

The manufacture of alcohol

Ethanol can easily be made from sugars and some starches by a fermentation process that involves the following reaction:

Glucose → Ethanol + Carbon dioxide
$C_6H_{12}O_6$ → $2C_2H_5OH$ + $2CO_2$

After about 36 hours the fermentation contains about 90 g of ethanol in every litre of solution. The yeast literally poisons itself with the alcohol at this concentration and so the mixture must be distilled to concentrate it.

In recent years ethanol has also been made from petroleum, though this would not solve an oil shortage! The ethene from the cracking process is combined with steam at a pressure of 40 atmospheres and a catalyst of phosphoric acid and alumina:

Ethene + Steam → Ethanol
C_2H_4 + H_2O → C_2H_5OH

The table shows the estimated proportion of ethanol manufactured by fermentation in the USA:

Year	1920	1935	1954	1963	1977	1982	1990
% manufactured	100	90	30	9	6.5	55	100

Answer the following questions, remembering that the alternative to fermentation is to use petroleum from crude oil:

1) Why do you think fermentation had become less important than ethene as a source of ethanol by the late 1970s?

2) Why do you think that fermentation has made a comeback in the 1980s?

3) Do you think ethanol could become a much more important chemical in the next century? Explain your answer.

MAKING A MODERN PETROL

In a petrol-driven car the petrol vapour is mixed with air and exploded. The explosion is started with an electrical spark from a sparking plug. What is the customer looking for in a good fuel? The customer expects the following of the engine:

- It must start on a cold morning.
- It must warm up quickly.
- It should respond quickly to the driver's controls.
- It should give good mileage.

The customer certainly does not want nasty noises from the engine or gummy deposits in the engine! To help prevent these, chemists try to ensure that petrol has the following properties:

- It forms enough vapour whether the temperature is freezing or hot, i.e. it is *volatile* over a large temperature range. This helps the engine to start when cold.
- It contains chemical additives to prevent the formation of gummy deposits.
- It has a high *octane rating* to give a very efficient explosion in the engine. A fuel with low octane rating tends to explode too violently on ignition. This violent explosion results in a metallic rattle in the engine. Until recently, lead compounds have always been added to petrol as a cheap way of boosting the octane rating. Lead compounds, however, are poisonous, and many people now feel that the level of lead compounds in the exhaust gases and the air is too high to be healthy. The presence of lead compounds in exhaust gases also contributes to pollution of the air in an indirect way. Vehicles can be fitted with an exhaust system containing a length of metal catalyst which is designed to remove harmful carbon monoxide and oxides of nitrogen. Lead compounds 'poison' this catalyst, i.e. prevent it from working, so that these gases pass into the air. The use of lead is gradually being phased out in the UK.

It would be easy to imagine that the gasoline (petrol) fraction from crude oil would be a good fuel. Unfortunately it contains straight-chain alkanes, which have a low octane rating. In practice the octane rating is boosted by adding (a) aromatic hydrocarbons and (b) alkanes that have a branched chain of carbon atoms. The reforming of the naphtha fraction makes both of these helpful types. The cracking of the heavier fractions also makes branched-chain alkanes.

Straight-chain alkane

Branched-chain alkane

The resulting petrol is a blend of hydrocarbons. It also contains detergent to clean the valves of the engine and the carburettor, and *glycols* to stop the petrol freezing in very cold conditions. In the future the octane rating may be increased by adding what the industry calls *oxygenates*. These are molecules such as alcohols and ethers, which contain oxygen as well as carbon and hydrogen. Their future use in place of aromatic hydrocarbons would leave these compounds (which are more expensive, and in relatively short supply) for other uses.

A SUCCESS STORY — THE MOSSMORRAN NGL PIPELINE

The Brent field, north-east of the Shetland Islands, contains many riches. It is estimated that it contains 3.5 billion billion cubic feet of methane. It also contains 530 million barrels of Natural Gas Liquid (NGL).

Shell and Esso collaborated with a plan to bring the methane and NGL to Mossmorran in Scotland. They decided on a pipeline for the 278 miles through the North Sea. This was to be followed by a 138 mile pipeline across land. The whole project is now complete and has jointly cost Shell and Esso £1000 million.

The 278 miles North Sea pipeline is called FLAGS (Far north Liquids and Associated Gas Systems). It carries the methane and NGL to St Fergus. The natural gas is separated, purified and dried, then sold to British Gas for the Natural Gas Grid. The natural gas from FLAGS will provide 12 per cent of all UK needs. The natural gas liquid travels from St Fergus to

Mossmorran to be separated into ethane, propane, butane and natural gasoline. The ethane goes to a cracker to be changed into more useful hydrocarbons. The others are loaded to customers at Braefoot Bay for shipment.

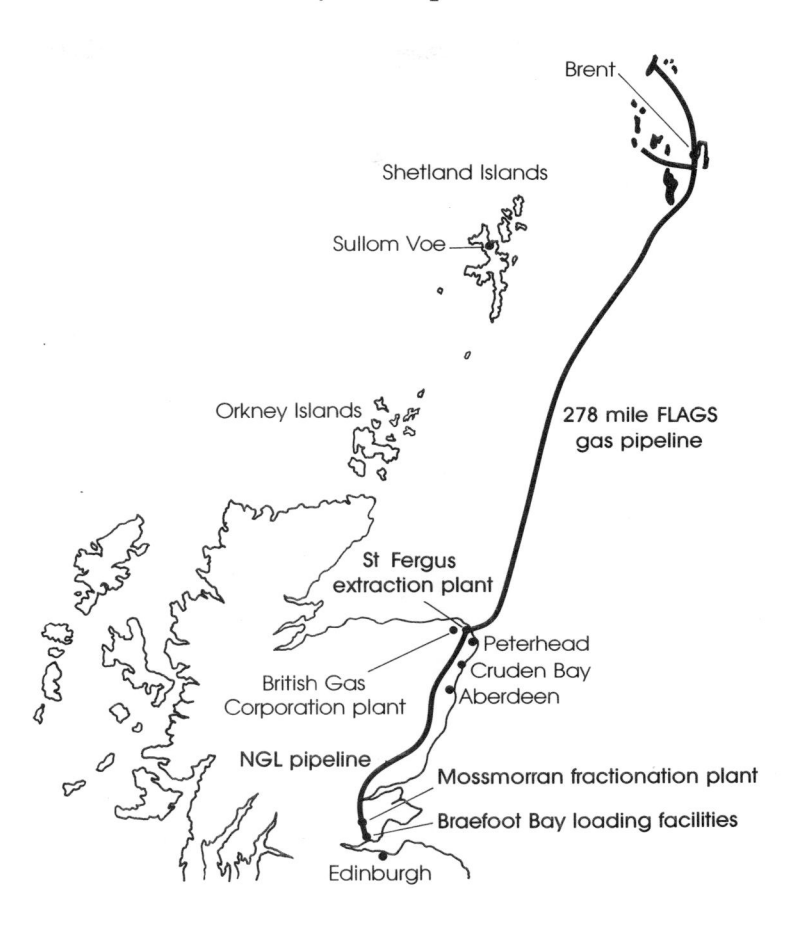

The Mossmorran Natural Gas Liquid pipeline

The St Fergus–Mossmorran pipeline is made of 20 inch diameter carbon steel, and has a coal-tar–enamel coating on the outside for protection. It is placed one to two metres below the surface, and crosses seven major rivers and two motorways. Wherever possible the environment has been improved by this project. There are isolation valves every 7.5 miles; these can be switched off automatically by computer if there is a leak. The whole length of the pipeline is inspected by helicopter every two weeks. The whole length of the pipeline on land will be checked closely each year.

The project is a great success. The pipeline transports 15 000 tonnes of NGL per day. The alternative would mean 500 tankers each carrying 30 tonnes on the road every day. A tanker would pass a given point on the route every 90 seconds!

COAL — FUEL OF THE FUTURE?

There is more coal in the world than oil and natural gas. The reserves of coal are vast. The coal deposits are spread over 80 countries, but almost 90 per cent is found in only four countries:

USSR	42%
USA	26%
China	13%
Australia	6%

Fuels used in the United Kingdom

Look at the graph of UK energy consumption and answer the questions:

1) Estimate the consumption of each fuel for the years 1960, 1965, 1975 and 1985. This is done by looking at a vertical line at the year and reading across, e.g. the coal consumed in 1960 is measured by the line AB, and the oil by BC.

2) In 1985 how much of the total oil used was from the North Sea?

3) Which fuels are becoming more popular? Suggest reasons for this popularity.

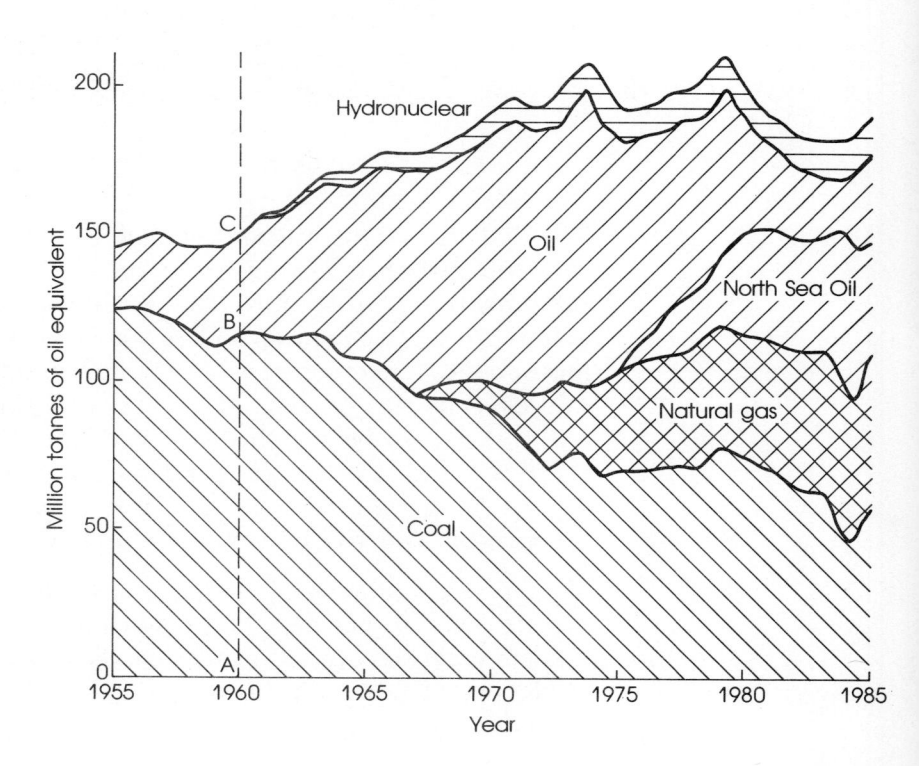

UK energy consumption, 1955–85

THE MODERN COAL MINE

The latest thing in coal mining is Advanced Technology Mining. The heavy-duty machines are computer-controlled and cost £3 million to £5 million each. They cut parallel tunnels in the coal seam to depths of about 1 metre. As the machine cuts it provides an unbroken ceiling of steel. This supports the roof and prevents the cave-ins which sometimes happen in mines. It automatically loads the cut coal on to a flexible steel conveyor belt. Operators are present down the mine but they are in safe positions.

A modern heavy-duty coal cutter

Computers control the conditions down the mine. They monitor ventilation, temperature and dangerous gas levels. Water tends to build up in mines. These water levels are also controlled by computer. The average depth of a mine-shaft in Britain is 450 metres. The deepest mine is 1000 metres. Lasers are now used to increase accuracy when sinking shafts and making tunnels.

CHEMICALS FROM COAL

Coal can supply most of the chemicals supplied by oil. It is simply a more difficult task to get the chemicals out. This is why oil is preferred as a source of chemicals. It is quite possible that new, easier methods may be developed for obtaining chemicals from coal.

The treasures that can be obtained from one tonne of coal

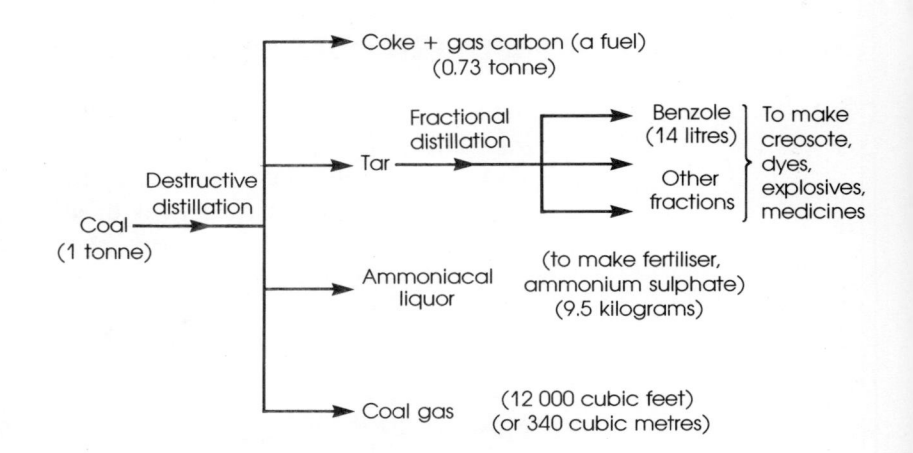

Coal (1 tonne) → Destructive distillation →
- Coke + gas carbon (a fuel) (0.73 tonne)
- Tar → Fractional distillation → Benzole (14 litres), Other fractions } To make creosote, dyes, explosives, medicines
- Ammoniacal liquor (to make fertiliser, ammonium sulphate) (9.5 kilograms)
- Coal gas (12 000 cubic feet) (or 340 cubic metres)

The chart above shows the chemicals obtained when coal is heated out of contact with air. The coal changes to coke and gives up ammoniacal liquor, coal tar and coal gas. This process is called *destructive distillation*. The ammoniacal liquor can be used to make ammonium sulphate, the fertiliser. The coal tar can be fractionally distilled to yield many useful fractions, the most important being benzole, made up of aromatic hydrocarbons. The coal gas is 50 per cent hydrogen, 30 per cent methane, with some carbon monoxide gas and other hydrocarbons. It is a good fuel, also known as 'town gas', because it was used to fuel homes and industry before natural gas came ashore.

Find (a) the weight of coke, (b) the volume of benzole, (c) the weight of fertiliser and (d) the volume of gas formed when 5 tonnes of coal is destructively distilled.

ACTIVITY 8

Destructive distillation of coal

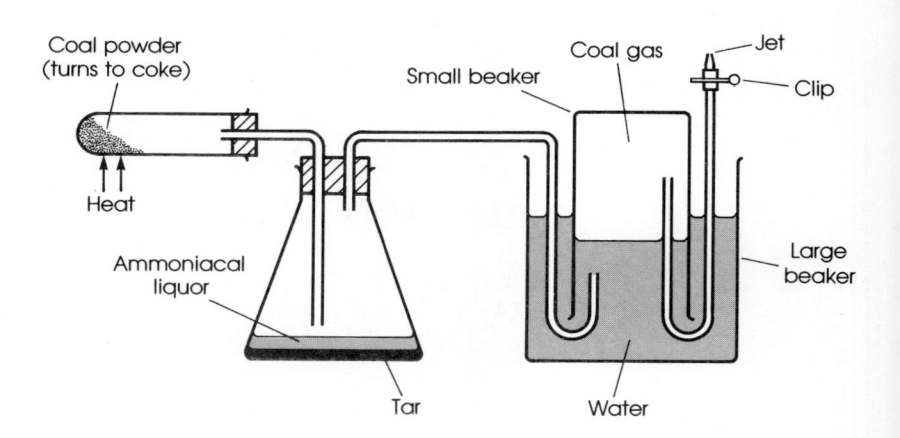

(To be demonstrated by the teacher)

1) Place some powdered coal in a Pyrex boiling-tube and set up the apparatus as shown.

2) Heat the coal with full flame and notice the products building up. After some time allow the apparatus to cool and inspect the products:
   (a) A water layer above the tar
   (b) Tar (which would be fractionally distilled in industry)
   (c) Coal gas. Release most of this into the air to prevent an explosion, and burn the rest at the jet,

FLUIDISED-BED COMBUSTION

In the UK coal has been used less by industry over the years. British Coal have been trying to develop more efficient ways of burning coal. This would reverse its decline in industry. Fluidised-bed combustion would seem to solve just this problem.

If a gradually increasing pressure of air is passed through solid particles, strange things happen. A certain pressure is reached when the solid appears to boil. It is then behaving just like a liquid. This is the principle used in fluidised-bed combustion. This is what happens:

1) There is a bed of coal-ash or sand at the base of the boiler.

2) Air is pumped into the bottom of the boiler through small holes in a plate.

3) The air pressure is adjusted to give the boiling effect.

4) Crushed coal is added (though recently the process has been made to work with uncrushed coal!).

5) The mixture is ignited and burns quickly at 950 °C. The heat converts the piped water into steam, which can be used to drive an electricity generator.

6) The ash made on burning the coal is removed continuously. This keeps the bed of ash at a constant level.

There are many advantages to this form of combustion:
- Even low-quality coal can be used, as can waste like wool, cotton or grease.
- It responds quickly to changing demands for steam.

- It burns things quickly and more efficiently because they mix so well as fluids.
- Control is easy with automatic coal and ash handling.
- There are no moving parts and so servicing is infrequent.
- The coal is burned in a totally enclosed system. This cuts down on pollution due to the gases sulphur dioxide and nitrogen oxides. Some limestone can be added to the boiler to help remove any sulphur dioxide formed.

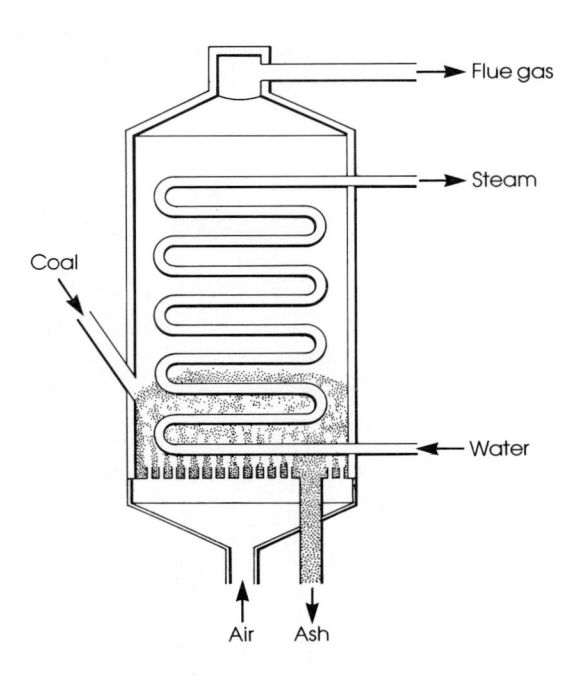

Fluidised-bed combustion

COAL-POWERED CARS

British Coal have plans to turn coal into petrol. They have had some success at their research laboratories in Cheltenham. Coal has been made into petrol, diesel fuel, jet fuel and chemicals. They have set up a pilot plant at Ayr in North Wales. This plant started in 1987 and converts 2.5 tonnes of coal a day. The process relies on solvents dissolving the coal. British Coal hope to convert 10 million tonnes of coal into petrol every year in the next century. The coal-powered car will be here to stay!

The process is called Liquid Solvent Extraction (LSE) and has the following stages:

1) Coal is crushed and dried, then mixed in a slurry with recycled oil.

2) The slurry is pumped to a digester at 400 °C. The solvent dissolves some of the coal here.

3) The liquid is filtered and the solution distilled into two fractions.

4) The lightest fraction is mixed with hydrogen and recycled to the slurry.

5) The heaviest fraction is mixed with hydrogen and cracked. This is called *hydrocracking*, and takes place at 465 °C and a pressure of 200 atmospheres.

6) The hydrocracked material is fractionally distilled to yield many useful products.

7) Some of the products are reformed to make petrol.

The AA prepare to exhibit a coal-powered car

EXERCISE

Rewrite these sentences including the missing words:

1 The _____ is the square hollow pipe that drives the drill _____. _____ helps to keep the _____ cool and guards against a _____ out.

2 Natural gas contains methane, _____, _____ and butane. These are all examples of _____. _____ oil is separated by the _____ distillation process. If alkenes are required a _____ of _____ oil must be _____.

3 The _____ has the greatest deposits of coal. When coal is heated out of contact with _____ it breaks up into solid _____ and two liquids, _____ and _____. The gas contains _____ and _____ and was used in homes as a _____ until natural gas was piped ashore.

4 A _____ survey is used to identify possible sites for oil. This is followed up by _____ samples. When the oil runs out it may be replaced by _____ to make all the organic chemicals. Then _____ of sugars will become much more important. Crude oil is a mixture of _____, _____ and aromatic compounds.

CROSSWORD

First, trace this grid on to a piece of paper (or photocopy this page — teacher, please see the note at the front of the book). Then fill in the answers. Do not write on this page.

Across

1 A type of plastic (3)
4 Chief hydrocarbons in oil (7)
8 The natural pool of oil (9)
10 Fish eggs to eat (3)
11 Please turn over (3)
13 Acidity — should be 4.5 for making alcohol (2)
14 Sonar acts like a human _____ (3)
16 An oil _____ supplies the oil (3)
19 The petroleum companies' organisation (4)
20 Plenty of this in Mossmorran (3)
24 Latest way to burn coal (9,3)
27 America (2)
28 Cycloalkanes to aromatics (9)
31 A _____ time for oil in Alaska (4)
32 Not a straight-chain alkane but a _____-alkane (5)
34 A biological catalyst (6)
35 Middle Eastern oil country (4)

Down

1 Glass-like plastic (7)
2 Oil for soap making (6)
3 Not soft detergent (4)
5 Our favourite sea for oil (5)
6 Famous oil company (5)
7 Solid left when coal is heated (4)
9 _____ oil has been purified (7)
12 Not the full-time army (2)
15 Copied (4)
17 It can say neigh (2)
18 Symbol for helium (2)
21 Welsh vegetable (4)
22 A mixture of oil with coal powder, for example (6)
23 The most solid oil fraction (7)
25 Application (3)
26 Total (3)
29 Your loose-leaf notes go well in this (4)
30 Butane has _____ carbon atoms (4)
33 The reverse of no (2)

CHAPTER 4
HOW LONG IS A MOLECULE? —PLASTIC POLYMERS

The idea of giant molecules was introduced by Professor Hermann Staudinger, a German chemist, in 1920. He said that giant molecules must contain at least *one thousand* atoms. He was awarded the Nobel prize for chemistry in 1953 for his work on giant molecules. We now call these molecules *polymers*.

There are many natural polymers such as proteins, cellulose and rubber. Chemists have copied these natural polymers, often making small changes to them. The polymers made by chemists are called *synthetic* polymers, most of which are *plastics*.

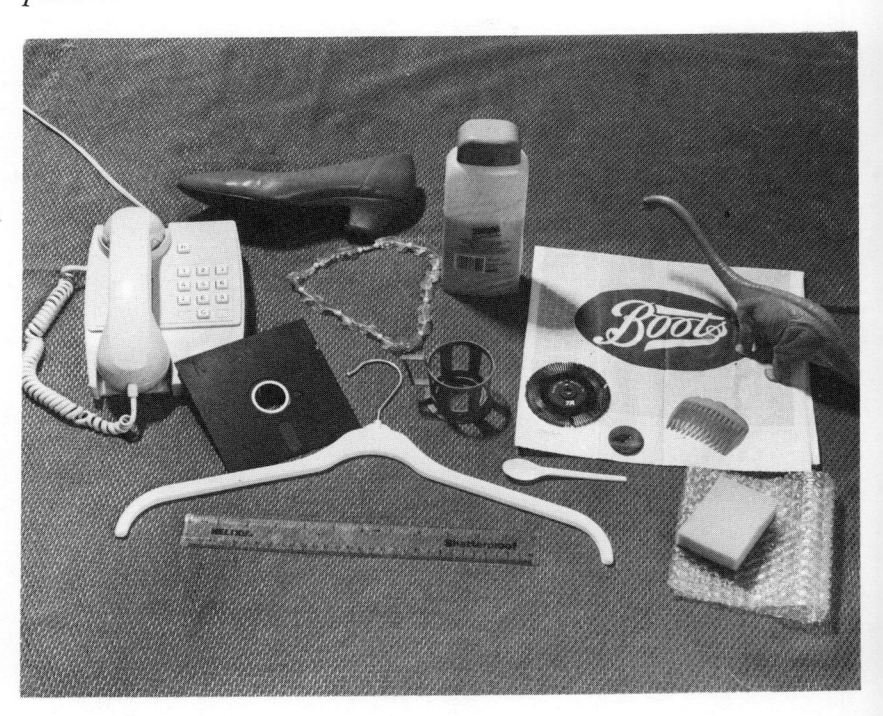

Plastics have become very important in the world. In 1985, some 74.5 million tonnes of plastic products were produced worldwide. Why have plastics become such popular materials? They can be strong, yet light (low density). Plastics will not corrode, as many metals do. Plastics are often cheaper than metals and more flexible. They are also much easier to process than many metals. With so many good points in their favour, no wonder plastics are increasing in popularity. Identify the plastic objects shown on the previous page.

TYPES OF PLASTIC

The flexibility, density and resistance to heat of a plastic depends on various factors:

- Whether the molecules contain branches off the main chain or not.
- Whether there are cross-links between polymer chains.
- The length of the polymer chains and the type of atoms included in them.

The next illustration shows various possible arrangements of the polymer molecules. Imagine the polymer molecules to be like strings of beads in which branches are also possible. The beads represent the atoms and the string represents the bonds between them.

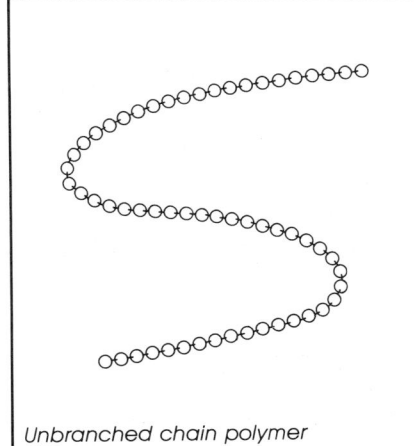

The arrangement of the polymer molecules determines the properties of the plastic

Unbranched chain polymer
High density because the molecules pack together. (If polythene the melting point is 135°C.)

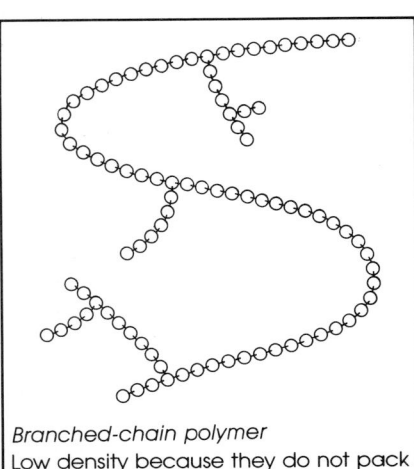

Branched-chain polymer
Low density because they do not pack well together with these branches. (If polythene the melting point is less than 135°C.)

67

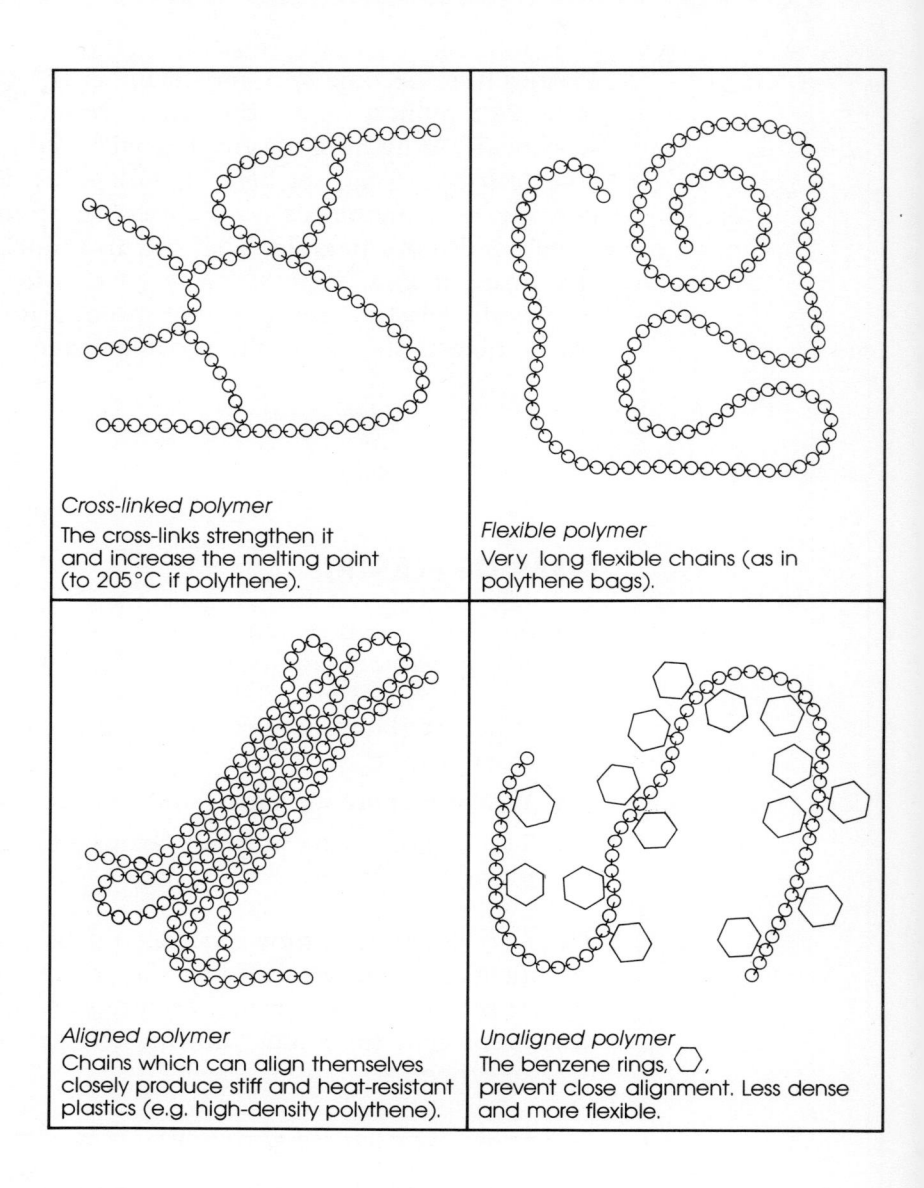

Cross-linked polymer
The cross-links strengthen it and increase the melting point (to 205 °C if polythene).

Flexible polymer
Very long flexible chains (as in polythene bags).

Aligned polymer
Chains which can align themselves closely produce stiff and heat-resistant plastics (e.g. high-density polythene).

Unaligned polymer
The benzene rings, ⬡, prevent close alignment. Less dense and more flexible.

There are three types of plastic:

- *Thermoplastics.* These are soft when heated and can be easily moulded. They harden again when cooled. There is little or no cross-linking in thermoplastics.
- *Thermosetting plastics.* These are hard and brittle at normal temperatures, owing to a great deal of cross-linking between the polymer molecules. They are heat-resistant and do not soften even at high temperatures. Once these plastics have been made they cannot be softened and remoulded.
- *Elastomers.* These have some cross-linking but less than there is in thermosetting plastics. They are rubbery in nature. They return to their former shape after they have been distorted.

Thermoplastics melt on heating.

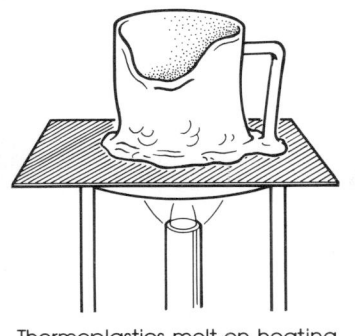

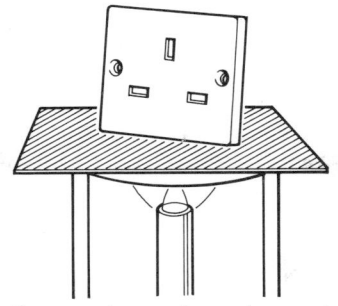

Thermosets remain unchanged at these temperatures.

Elastomers regain their shape after distortion, i.e. they are elastic.

Three types of plastic

HOW ARE PLASTICS MADE?

The polymer chemist starts with the units. These are called *monomers*. Many of these monomers are based on *ethene*. The ethene is obtained from crude oil by the cracking process (p. 50). The most important feature of the ethene molecule is the double bond between the two carbon atoms. This is the key to how the monomers join to make a polymer, because one bond may break, allowing other molecules to add on. You will see that one hydrogen atom has an asterisk (*) next to it. Replacing this atom with a different atom or group, e.g. chlorine makes the world of difference to the type of plastic obtained.

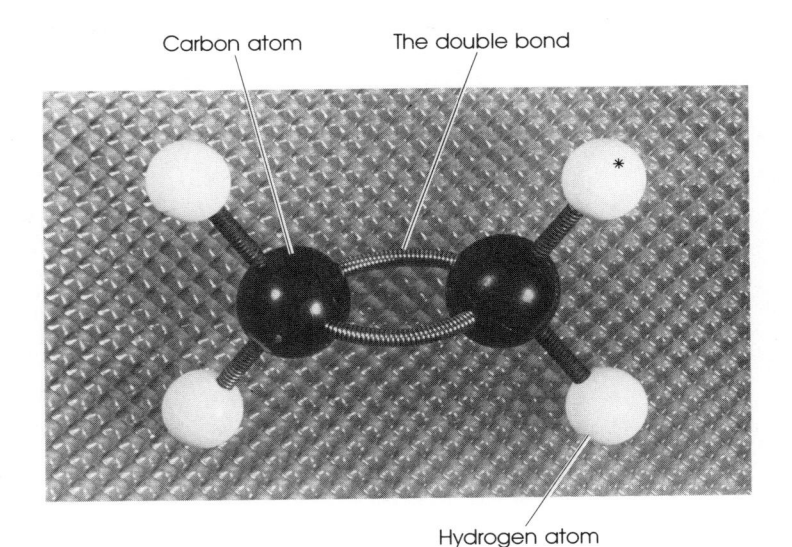

Carbon atom

The double bond

The ethene molecule

Hydrogen atom

You will almost certainly recognise the names of some common polymers: PVC, polythene and polystyrene are familiar names. Perspex® is an *acrylic* plastic and looks like glass. It is used in some double glazing. Teflon® is the non-stick plastic used to coat the insides of many kitchen utensils.

Addition polymerisation

Monomers → *Polymers (plastics)*

Ethene → Polythene

Vinyl chloride → Polyvinyl chloride (PVC)

There is another type of polymerisation (making polymers) known as *condensation*. Nylon and Terylene® are both condensation polymers. They are called condensation polymers because small molecules such as water or ammonia are lost during the making of the polymer.

Plastics are made in various ways but often a catalyst is used. Sometimes a higher pressure than normal atmospheric pressure is also used. Polythene can be made in two different ways, according to the properties required. The monomer ethene is the starter for each process:

Low density polythene	*High density polythene*
Pressure 2000 times that of the atmosphere.	Near normal atmospheric pressure.
No catalyst.	Special catalyst (Titanium (IV) chloride)
Many branches in the polymer so they fit together badly. Result: low density.	Few branches in the polymer so they fit together well. Result: high density.
A soft plastic.	A harder plastic.
Made by English chemists Fawcett and Gibson in 1933.	Made by German chemist Ziegler in 1955.
Uses: 'cling-film' to cover food, small flexible bottles, insulation against heat loss.	Uses: Petrol tanks, bottle crates, pipes that will withstand pressure.

WHAT DO THEY DO TO PLASTICS?

Extrusion, injection moulding, calendering and *foaming* are the four main things that are done to plastics to make the objects we see every day. The first three of these processes are summarised in the illustrations below.

Extrusion is used to make pipes or sheets of plastic

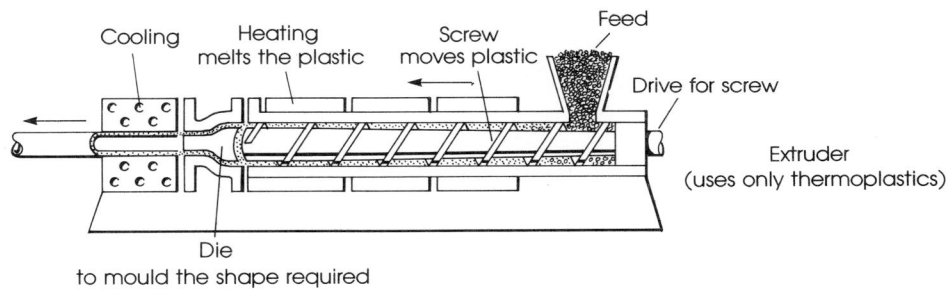

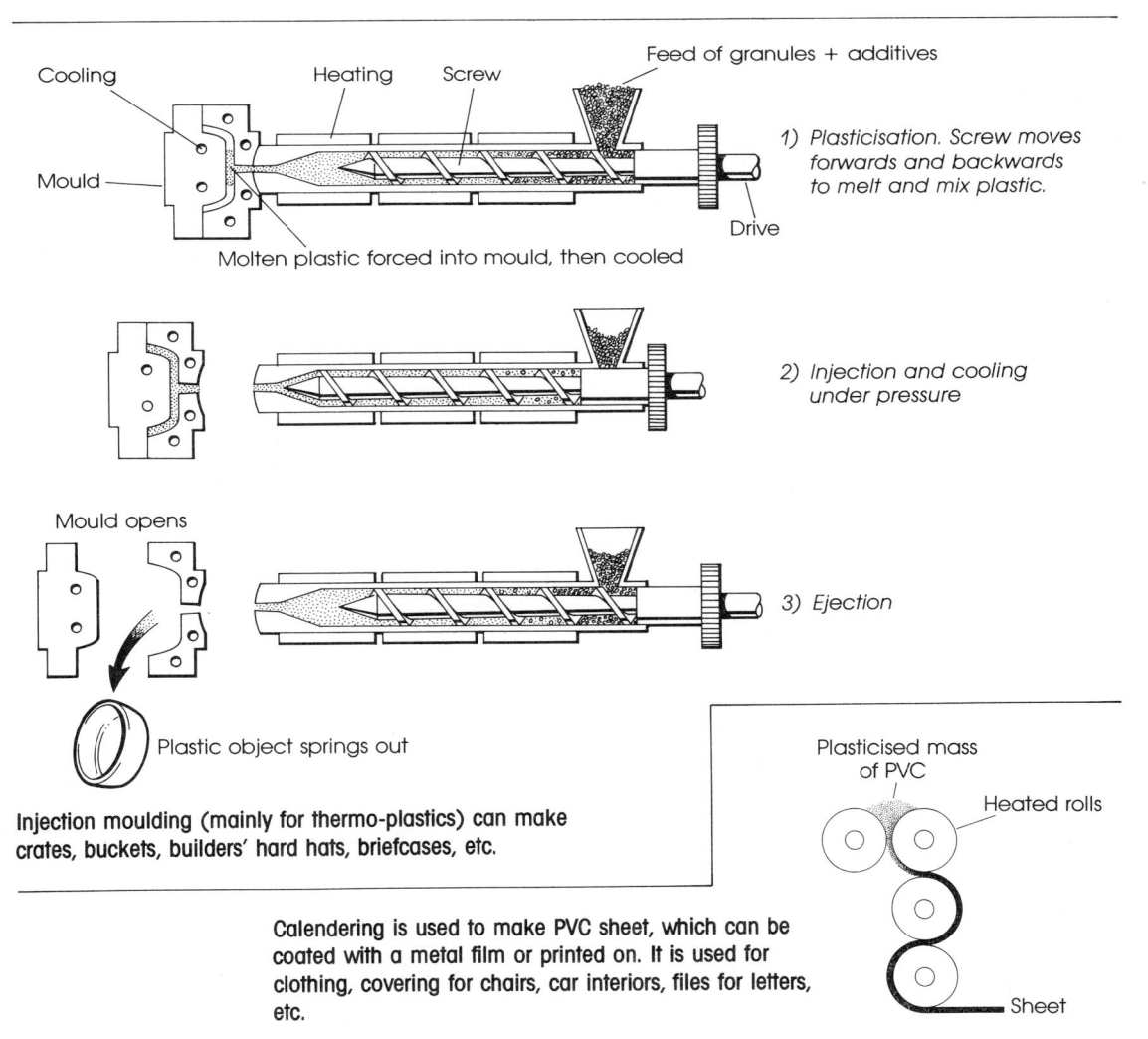

Cooling — Heating melts the plastic — Screw moves plastic — Feed — Drive for screw

Extruder (uses only thermoplastics)

Die to mould the shape required

Cooling — Heating — Screw — Feed of granules + additives

Mould

Molten plastic forced into mould, then cooled

Drive

1) Plasticisation. Screw moves forwards and backwards to melt and mix plastic.

2) Injection and cooling under pressure

Mould opens

3) Ejection

Plastic object springs out

Injection moulding (mainly for thermo-plastics) can make crates, buckets, builders' hard hats, briefcases, etc.

Plasticised mass of PVC — Heated rolls — Sheet

Calendering is used to make PVC sheet, which can be coated with a metal film or printed on. It is used for clothing, covering for chairs, car interiors, files for letters, etc.

In the fourth method (foaming) the molten plastic is turned into a foam, then cooled. The foam may be created by passing compressed air into the molten plastic, or by the use of a *blowing agent*. Such an agent is sodium hydrogencarbonate. This is mixed with the solid plastic and heated, and is broken down by the heat, giving off carbon dioxide. This gas forms bubbles in the molten plastic, which remain on cooling. A foam plastic is less dense and a better insulator against heat losses. One famous foam plastic is 'expanded polystyrene' which is used for ceiling tiles, packaging and drinking-beakers. Sponges are also made by foaming.

ADDITIVES TO POLYMERS

The quality of plastics can be improved by adding certain chemicals. *Stabilisers* are added to improve the resistance of plastics to heat and light. *Plasticisers* are added to improve the flexibility of plastics. *Fillers*, such as wood, flour, clay and small glass beads, are often also added. The filler reduces the cost of the plastic and makes it easier to process. Sometimes fibre-fillers such as carbon and asbestos are added. These increase the stiffness and strength of the plastic.

BIODEGRADABLE PLASTICS

Plastic waste is a major problem and one that will not go away! The majority of plastics remain in the environment because they are not *biodegradable*, i.e. they are not broken down naturally by microbes in the environment. Plastics are so cheap that it may not be worth recycling them. If they are burned they produce dangerous gases. Scientists are perfecting two types of biodegradable plastic:

- *Starch-filled plastic*. It is known that thermoplastics become brittle and fracture when buried for many years. This would happen much more quickly if the surface area of the plastic were increased. Small amounts of starch in the plastic act as food for bacteria and fungi if moisture is present. As the starch is eaten, the plastic breaks up, giving a larger surface area. Sometimes an oxidant is also included in the plastic and this hastens the decay of the plastic.
- *Bacterial thermoplastic*. ICI have developed a plastic that is made by bacteria. It is a polyester called poly-3-hydroxybutyrate (PHB). The bacteria grow in large tanks containing a substrate such as sugars or alcohol or carbon

dioxide and hydrogen. The bacteria make large quantities of PHB granules. This plastic is completely biodegradable when bacteria, fungi or algae attack. Such attack will always happen in soil, rivers, lakes and the sea.

ACTIVITY 9

A project you could do

Make a study of the plastic waste from households. Is it all necessary? Is a lot of packaging simply for presentation? Would returnable glass bottles be better than plastic bottles? Should we keep different types of household wastes in separate bins to help recycling?

A SUCCESS STORY — PLASTIC WASTE BACK TO OIL

We know that plastics come from oil and that oil is a precious liquid. Every time a plastic article is discarded it is as though some oil were thrown away. Scientists have now found a way to convert waste plastic into oil.

The plastic waste can be broken down by heat in the absence of oxygen from the air. This is called *pyrolysis*, and temperatures of up to 800 °C are used. Half of the vapour formed as the plastic decomposes is used to heat the pyrolysis machine. The remaining vapour is condensed to give valuable oil. The oil obtained is more valuable than the energy

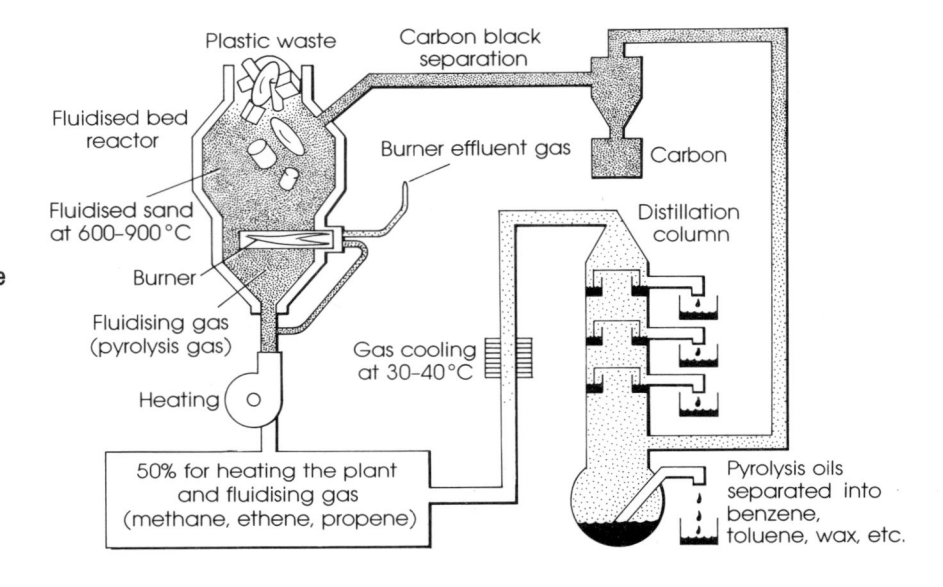

Recycling plastic waste into oil by pyrolysis

obtained by burning the plastic. The diagram shows a machine that can handle 8000 tonnes of plastic waste each year. It is an expensive process but it is saving on our limited oil resources. Even if it costs money it always pays to recycle unless we are happy to run out of chemicals in the next century.

DATA ON PLASTICS

1) The following figures show the percentage use of plastics, by weight, in the UK. Use the data to construct a pie chart.

Use	Percentage by weight
Packaging	36
Building	21
Electrical/electronic	10
Transport	5
Furniture	5
Toys and leisure	4
Housewares	2.5
Agriculture	2
Clothing and footware	1
Medical products	1
Others	12.5

2) The following figures show the energy required (measured as tonnes of oil that must be burned) to make one cubic metre of material. Use the data to make a bar graph.

Material	Energy
Aluminium	15
Copper	11
Steel	5
PVC	1.2
Polyethene (either density)	0.8
Polystyrene	0.5

The prices for one cubic metre of these materials do not follow the pattern of energy required. What other factors contribute to the price asked for a material?

ACTIVITY 10

Heat conductivity test

You are required to design an experiment to show which material is the better conductor of heat: metal or plastic. You are supplied with the apparatus shown on the next page. Think up an experiment which will enable you to answer the question.

Write a plan. Show the plan to your teacher. If he or she approves, put your plan into action.

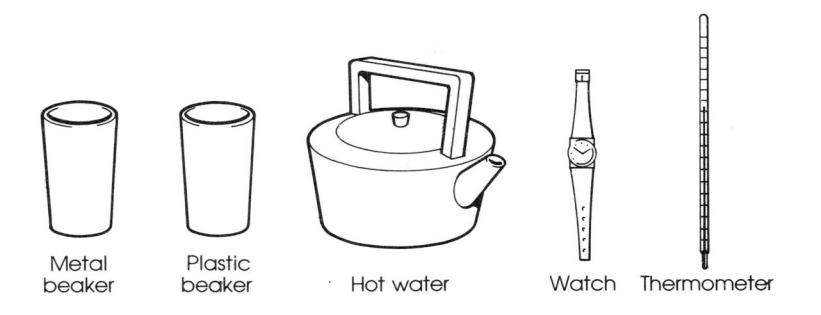

Metal beaker | Plastic beaker | Hot water | Watch | Thermometer

Further ideas

1) Find how to make the acrylic plastic Perspex® (work in a fume-cupboard).
2) Make cellulose acetate from paper.
3) Make models of polymers using ball-and-spring kits.

EXERCISE

Rewrite the following sentences supplying the correct word(s) in the spaces:

1 Plastics are used for a multitude of things because they have ____ combined with low density. They are poor conductors of ____ and ____, and are therefore known as insulators. They are not ____ by chemicals and so do ____ corrode. They are ____ when compared with many metals.

2 Plastic waste does not ____ when discarded, unlike most other waste. Some can be ____ by pyrolysis but this is ____. Plastic waste gives energy when ____.

3 The starting substances used to make ____ are called monomers. Ethene is one of the simplest monomers and makes the plastic called ____. If an atom of ____ replaces one hydrogen atom in this monomer, the plastic PVC is made. ____ and condensation are the two ways to make a polymer.

4 Polymers on their ____ often lack the good properties required. ____ such as stabilisers, ____ and ____ are often added to plastics to improve them. Plastics can be processed in various ways: into sheets by ____, into pipes by ____ or shaped by injection-____.

5 The three main types of plastic are ____, ____ and elastomers. ____ can be melted and moulded whilst ____ cannot be melted. Elastomers ____ to their original shape after ____.

CHAPTER 5
THE FARMER'S FRIENDS — FERTILISERS AND PESTICIDES

WHAT ARE FERTILISERS?

Plants will only grow well in soil if they have light, air, water and certain salts (nutrients) which are soluble in water. The main chemical elements that plants require, in one form or another, are nitrogen, phosphorus and potassium. The best fertilisers contain these elements in abundance. Some fertilisers contain only one or two of these elements and some contain other elements that plants require in small amounts (trace elements).

Trade name of fertiliser	*Formula*
Sulphate of ammonia	$(NH_4)_2SO_4$
Urea	$(NH_2)_2CO$
Single superphosphate	$Ca_3(PO_4)_2$ and $CaSO_4$
Triple superphosphate	$Ca_3(PO_4)_2$ and $(NH_4)_3PO_4$
Sulphate of potash	K_2SO_4
Basic slag	$Ca_3(PO_4)_2$ and $CaSiO_3$ and CaO + trace elements
NPK	NH_4NO_3 and KCl and $(NH_4)_3PO_4$

Spot which of the main essential elements are present in each of the above fertilisers.

For the manufacture of NPK fertiliser see Extending Science 6: *Land and Soil* by R E Lee (ST(P)).

ACTIVITY 11

To show that powders may be granulated by the addition of a liquid

(a) Dissolve as much ammonium sulphate solid in 100 cm³ of distilled water as possible. This makes a saturated solution.

(b) Add 50 g of fine silica sand (or washed scouring powder) to the solution in a polythene bag. Seal the bag.

(c) Knead the mixture thoroughly in the polythene bag. Transfer the mixture to a conical flask and shake vigorously. Spread the product thinly on a paper sheet and dry in an oven. Look at the granules, using a microscope if necessary. This is similar to the granulation stage in the manufacture of the fertiliser NPK.

WHY ARE FERTILISERS NEEDED?

In normal circumstances soil naturally contains sufficient quantities of all the elements that plants need, but the repeated harvesting of crops removes large amounts of these, with the result that crop yields decrease.

The rapid rise in population is the key to the need for fertilisers. All the people must be fed. The soil can only produce enough crops if fertiliser is added. If the population of the UK were 30 million (as it was in 1876) instead of the present 55 million, then no fertilisers would be required to feed the population.

The processes that naturally remove and return nitrogen to the soil are known as the *nitrogen cycle*. For details see Extending Science 1: *Air* by E N Ramsden and R E Lee and Extending Science 6: *Land and Soil* by R E Lee (ST(P)).

Fertilisers play their part in the farmer's production of food

The natural nitrogen cycle needs our help in the form of fertilisers because it is being upset by:

- Farmland being used for building instead of producing crops, thus reducing the area available to take nitrogen from air
- Valuable soil being washed and blown away because of removal of trees and hedgerows (soil erosion)
- Plants being harvested and eaten rather than being allowed to decay naturally and return nitrogen to the soil
- Water washing (leaching) nitrates out of the soil and into rivers and streams

Estimated world figures for routes by which nitrogen gets into the soil for the year 1980 are:

Route	Million Tonnes of Nitrogen
Lightning in the atmosphere	25
Nitrogen oxides from vehicle exhausts*	20
Bacterial action in soil (also death decay and excretion)	80
Bacterial action in water	20
Fertilisers*	60

(* = unnatural process)

Use the chart to estimate:

- The total nitrogen converted unnaturally
- The total nitrogen converted naturally
- What fraction of the nitrogen comes from the unnatural sources

How do you think the last answer will change as the years progress?

DO FERTILISERS REALLY WORK?

ACTIVITY 12

The effect of nutrients on plant growth

Make up solutions of the following:

Sodium nitrate containing 2 g/l
Potassium chloride containing 2 g/l
Sodium dihydrogenphosphate containing 0.2 g/l

1) Make up four identical pots with equal quantities of freshly washed sand.

2) Add 0.5 g of grass seed to each.

3) Water pot 1 with the sodium nitrate solution only, pot 2 with potassium chloride only, and pot 3 with sodium dihydrogenphosphate only.

4) Water pot 4 with a mixture of all three solutions.

5) Cut the grass in each pot to a height of 25 mm each week. Weight the cuttings from each. Which pot shows the best growth?

Find out the effect of using (a) more concentrated, (b) less concentrated solutions.

As a rough guide, a tonne of nitrogen-containing fertiliser produces fifteen tonnes of grain; this is a spectacular gain by any measure. A research station in Rothamsted, Essex, has compared crop yields with and without fertilisers for 140 years. The results for 1980 to 1982 are shown below:

Dose of fertiliser calculated by element (kilograms/hectare)			*Yield of crop (tonnes/hectare)*	
Nitrogen	Phosphorus	Potassium	Wheat	Potatoes
0	0	0	1.69	8.47
96	0	0	3.68	8.30
0	77	107	2.04	16.63
96	77	107	6.60	38.57

Use the data to answer these questions:

1) Which of the two crops particularly thrives on nitrogen? Comment on the result for nitrogen with the other crop.

2) Which crop shows the best percentage increase in yield for the phosphorus/potassium fertiliser? Is the other crop also favoured by this fertiliser?

3) For the nitrogen/phosphorus/potassium fertiliser, divide the yield by the 'no fertiliser' yield for each crop. Which shows the best fractional increase? What is particularly noticeable about the yields for this fertiliser?

ARE FERTILISERS COST-EFFECTIVE?

Fertilisers repay their cost many times over. Examine the graph linking the yield of winter wheat to the amount of nitrogen fertiliser applied to the soil, and answer the questions:

1) How many kilograms of nitrogen fertiliser must be applied to a hectare of land to double the yield obtained with no fertiliser?

2) What is the maximum dose of fertiliser worth applying to the soil to obtain a maximum yield of winter wheat?

3) Why is a farmer unwise to apply 300 g of fertiliser per hectare when growing winter wheat?

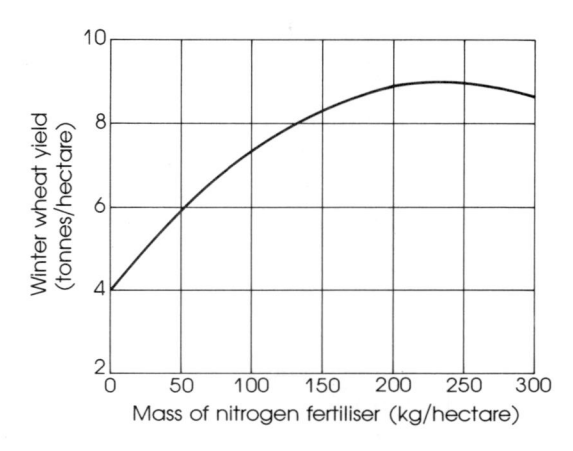

Variation of crop yield with amount of fertiliser applied

A further result from Rothamsted shows the way costs for the farmer drop drastically with fertiliser application:

		Without fertiliser	With fertiliser
Fertiliser treatment (kg/hectare)	Nitrogen	0	97
	Phosphorus	0	77
	Potassium	0	107
Cost to farmer (£/hectare)	Wheat	479	575
	Potatoes	1468	1564
Yield of crops (tonnes/hectare)	Wheat	1.69	6.60
	Potatoes	8.47	38.57
Total cost of crops (£/tonne)	Wheat	283	87
	Potatoes	173	41

Answer the questions on this table:

1) Look at the 'cost to farmer' row and work out the cost of the fertiliser.

2) Look at the farmer's total cost per tonne of crop and work out the decrease in cost using fertiliser for each crop in (a) £s and (b) percentage terms.

ARE THERE PROBLEMS WITH FERTILISERS?

You can always find experts who disagree with one another. The story so far suggests that fertilisers are a great boon. Unfortunately there are some worrying aspects of their use. Some farmers may be over-using fertilisers, though economically this does not make sense. There is an argument that says farmers are producing too much food and should cut down on fertilisers.

The level of nitrates is building up in our water supplies. In many parts of the UK the level exceeds the maximum admissible concentration of 50 milligrams of nitrate per litre set by the European Economic Community (EEC). It seems that nitrate fertiliser applied to the land is being leached by rain into our water supplies.

Some experts believe that nitrates are related to stomach cancer. Whilst this has been proven in test animals there is little evidence in humans. A very rare blood disease in young babies, known as 'blue baby syndrome', has been connected with nitrate levels in water. Once again there is a lot of doubt about the connection.

There are also some who think that fertilisers eventually destroy the soil structure. Such people favour natural fertilisers like horse manure because these actually improve the structure of the soil. The manures do not contain the suspect nitrate either. Organic farming is all about using natural manures and no pesticides for crops. The organically farmed produce is more expensive but a growing number of people prefer the taste of these 'natural' crops.

The nitrogen and phosphorus of fertilisers leached by rain water into lakes act as food for weeds. The weeds take over and use up all of the dissolved oxygen when they decay. This means that nothing else can live in the lake. Large parts of Lake Erie in North America have this problem, known as *eutrophication*.

THE FARMER AT WAR — THE FIGHT AGAINST PESTS

The farmer must wage a constant war against pests to gain a good crop yield. Up to 30 per cent of all crops are lost to pests. Even more valuable food would be lost without the use of chemicals. The term 'pest' includes weeds, insects, fungi, slugs and snails, rodents such as rats and mice, eelworms, and mites. *Pesticides* are the chemicals used to kill off or control these pests, and they fall into several categories.

Fungus

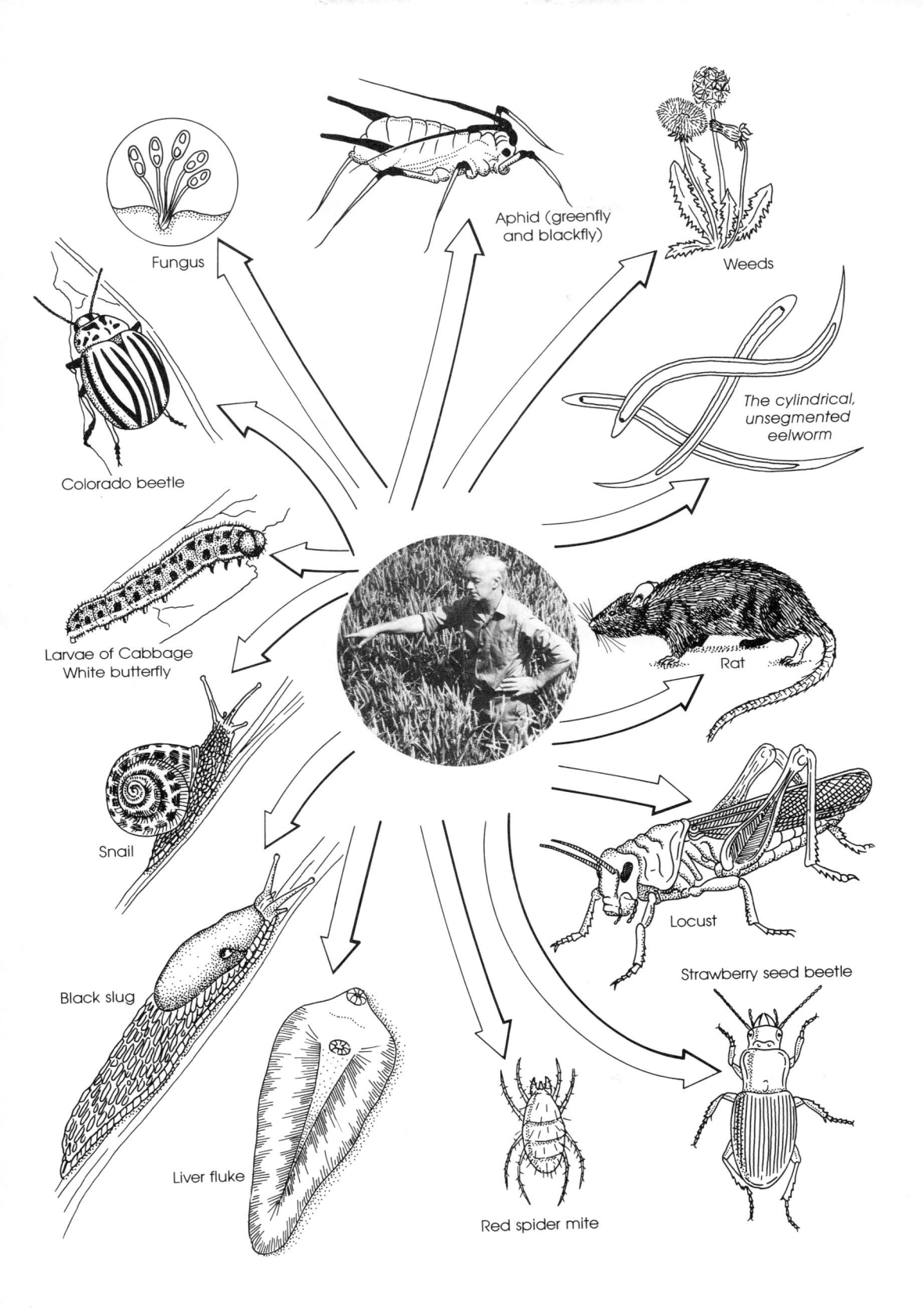

Aphid (greenfly and blackfly)

Weeds

Colorado beetle

The cylindrical, unsegmented eelworm

Larvae of Cabbage White butterfly

Rat

Snail

Locust

Black slug

Strawberry seed beetle

Liver fluke

Red spider mite

The farmer at war

Herbicides

These are used to kill or control weeds. You will know from looking at gardens that the unwelcome plants, known as weeds, seem to be able to survive any conditions; they seem to be stronger than our cultivated plants. Weeds are pests because they compete with the growing crops for water, light and nutrients in the soil. The weeds may also act as 'home' for unwanted crop pests and diseases and pass them on in the next growing season.

Herbicides may be 'total' or 'selective' in their action. The 'total' variety destroys all vegetation and is likely to be used to clear the land after harvesting the crop. The 'selective' variety can kill weeds in a crop without harming the crop.

In the UK herbicides are in more demand than any other pesticide. Tropical areas such as Africa and Asia have fewer problems with weeds competing with their crops.

Herbicides may act in one or more of three ways on the weed:

Contact Herbicides. These control weeds by scorching or destroying the green matter (chlorophyll). This type of herbicide kills by contact with the outside of the plant. For this reason it must be spread over as much of the surface of the plant as possible.

Translocated Herbicides. These are absorbed into the plant system and are carried out by the plant's 'juices' to other parts of the plant. They are slower in action than the contact herbicides.

Residual Herbicides. These control weeds as they start to grow (germinate). They are applied to the soil at the time the crop is planted. They act as a barrier of chemical in the top layer of soil, and as the weeds germinate their young roots absorb the chemical and are controlled by it.

Types of herbicide

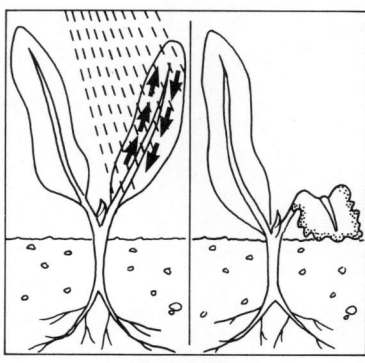

Contact herbicide | Translocated herbicide | Residual herbicide

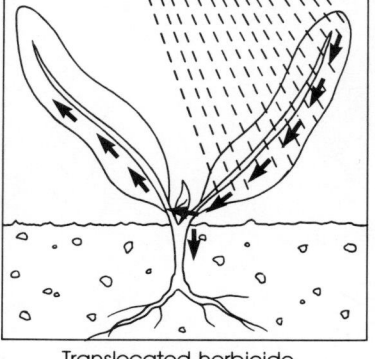

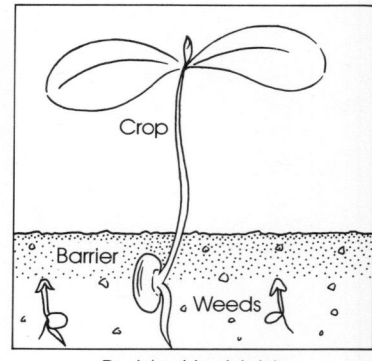

Insecticides

These are used to control or kill insects. They are second to herbicides on the world pesticide market. Tropical countries suffer particularly from insects. A large swarm of locusts can consume 3000 tonnes of green crops in a day! There are about a million known species of insect, but fortunately for us only about 10 000 of these are regarded as pests. Many insects are actually helpful because they feed on pests.

Other insects can carry diseases that attack humans. For example, the mosquito carries malaria, the body louse carries typhus and the tsetse fly carries sleeping sickness. Insecticides may be classified by the way they act in insects:

Contact Insecticides. These kill on contact, and so must be sprayed on the insects or sprayed where the insects will walk. DDT is an example of a contact insecticide.

Systemic Insecticides. These are absorbed by growing plants and distributed inside them. Any insects which feed on the plants by a sucking action take in some insecticide. Aphids (greenfly etc.) can be controlled in this way.

Stomach Ingestion Insecticides. These insecticides kill because the insects eat some of the chemical previously sprayed on the plants.

Fumigant Insecticides. The fumes given off by the insecticide are taken into the breathing mechanism of the insect. The chemical usually affects the nervous system of the insect. Nicotine is an example of a natural fumigant insecticide.

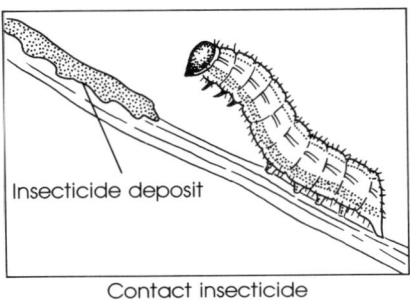

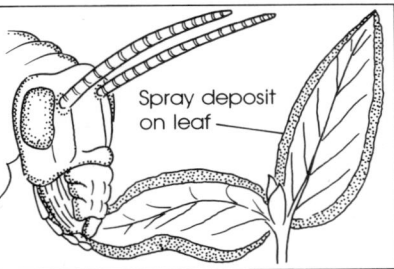

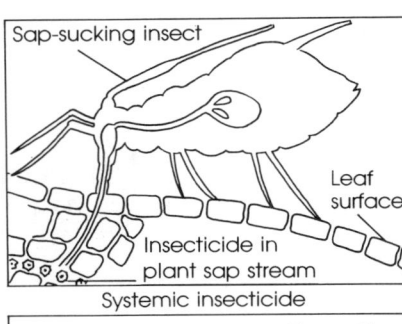

Types of insecticide

Fungicides

These kill off or control fungi that will harm plants. Of the 100 000 or so species of fungi known only about 200 are known to cause serious plant disease. A fungal disease known as 'potato blight' was responsible for the destruction of the complete potato crop in Ireland in 1840. Fungal disease is still a problem, and results in crop losses in the region of £60 billion a year.

Molluscicides

These control slugs and snails. They are usually mixed with a bait such as bran to attract the pests. The slug or snail will eat the mixture and gain a fatal dose of the insecticide.

The liver fluke is a pest which attacks sheep and cattle on the farm. The life cycle of the liver fluke involves snails and so a molluscicide is able to kill this pest.

Nematicides

These kill eelworms (known as *nematodes*). The eelworms are invisible to the naked eye but attack the roots of crops.

Acaricides

These kill very small mites, such as the red spider.

Ovicides

These are used to kill the eggs of various insects and mites. Controlling the eggs can prevent a build-up of the pest the following season.

Rodenticides

These are chemicals that kill rats and mice.

The table below shows the sales of pesticides in the UK for the year 1983:

Type of Pesticide	*Sales in the UK (£ million)*	*Exports (£ million)*
Fungicides	77.3	27
Herbicides	188.3	215.1
Insecticides	30.8	103.3
Others	32.9	16.2

Use the table to answer these questions:

1) Find the total sales of pesticides (a) in the UK, (b) in exports. Do we export much more than we consume?
2) Which type of pesticide has the greatest sale in the UK and the greatest export sale?
3) Which types of pesticide are included in 'others' in the chart?
4) Which pesticides are kept mainly for UK use?

MAKING A PESTICIDE

Imagine that you have the problem of making a pesticide to control caterpillars. Let us suppose it will act by attacking the caterpillar's stomach. What should the properties of such a pesticide be?

- It should not kill domestic animals or humans when taken in by accident.
- It should not be poisonous to the crop being protected, e.g. cabbage.
- It should not break down in sunlight or be washed away by rain.
- It should not repel the caterpillar.
- It should not break down in acidic or alkaline conditions.
- It should not be rendered harmless by chemicals in the plant or in the caterpillar.
- It must be able to travel along the gut of the caterpillar to its stomach.
- It should have no effect on the 'good' insects or other life forms.
- It will not start to act in the soil, only in the caterpillar.

With all these properties to consider it is difficult work making a pesticide. It can take up to seven years to produce a new pesticide. Pressure from those worried about the effect of pesticides on the countryside has forced this long, costly programme. As a result, the number of new pesticides coming on to the market has dropped markedly.

The programme of making a new pesticide can be divided into three stages:

Stage 1. The chemical is made and tested in the laboratory, the greenhouse and then on a small scale in open fields. Some tests are made to see if the compound is poisonous. Results are sent to the Pesticide Safety Precautions Scheme (PSPS). This stage takes two to three years and represents 20 per cent of the total cost.

Stage 2. This only takes place if the PSPS gives trials clearance for the first stage. There are small scale farm trials, checks on what the pesticide contains, tests to find what happens to the pesticide in plants and soil, and also measurements to find how long residues of the pesticide stay in the soil. Tests to see whether the pesticide is a long-term poison are made together with feeding tests. Again the PSPS must be notified of the results. This stage takes one to two years and accounts for 30 per cent of the total cost.

Stage 3. If the first two stages have been passed, limited sales of the pesticide are allowed. This third stage involves only a few tests, but these are very detailed and very expensive. There are large-scale farm trials coupled with long-term research and development of the pesticide. The PSPS check that hazards to users of the pesticide and wildlife are reduced to an acceptable level. The Agricultural Chemicals Approval Scheme (ACAS) must then check that the product is as efficient in its particular application as is claimed by the manufacturers. This stage takes one to two years and accounts for 50 per cent of the total cost.

A pesticide manufacturer will spend something like £6 million to produce one successful new pesticide. This high cost reflects the fact that about 15 000 compounds are tested to get one that passes today's stringent rules.

CONCERN ABOUT PESTICIDES

Many concerned about the environment have voiced fears about the side-effects of pesticides. Cancer, birth deformities in children and destruction of wildlife have been blamed on pesticides.

Certainly DDT was found to interfere with the utilisation of calcium in birds. As a result the birds' eggshells were too thin and rarely resulted in young being successfully hatched. DDT has also been shown to collect in fatty tissue and to concentrate in the food chain leading to humans. DDT residues stay in the soil for a very long time, and are therefore potentially very dangerous. DDT has now been banned in most countries.

A pesticide called 2,4,5,T ('Agent Orange') has also been linked to birth deformities and cancer, and in December 1987 a pesticide, cyhexatin, widely used on fruit farms for 15 years, was banned by the UK.

FUTURE CONTROL OF PESTS

With environmental worries, scientists may turn to safer methods of controlling pests:

- *Predator farms.* The ladybird is a predator that loves eating harmful greenfly, and could be specially bred to do this job. Other predators could be encouraged in this way.
- *Pheromones.* These are chemicals that insects give off to attract the opposite sex. If the chemical is extracted it can be used to lure the insects to a particular spot. The insects are then destroyed or irradiated to stop them from reproducing.
- *Microbes.* Microbes can be modified by biotechnologists. These special strains of microbe feed on a substrate and produce pesticides. The pesticides turn out to be superior to many produced by other methods.
- *Disease resistance.* Great strides are being made in breeding new varieties of plant. It may be possible to breed crops with so much resistance to disease that they do not need the protection offered by pesticides.
- *Food from alternative sources.* It is thought that much food will in future by made by using small living organisms. They will grow and multiply in a liquid such as oil, then be harvested and used as food. This is biotechnology, and one day may be the major source of food. There will then be little use for pesticides.

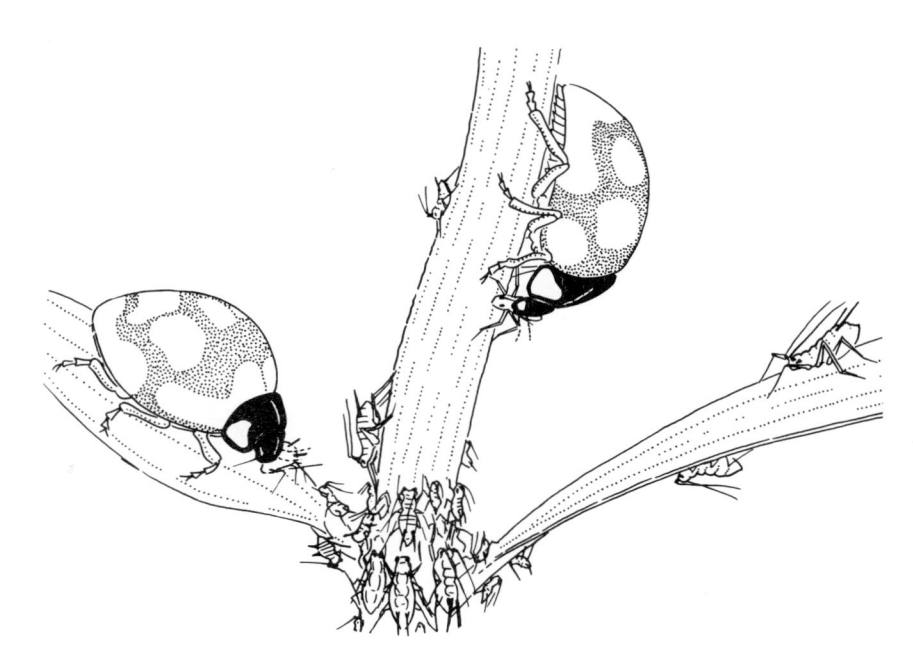

Ladybirds—a natural pesticide

EXERCISE

Rewrite the following sentences adding the missing words:

1 The three vital elements for a fertiliser are ____, phosphorus and ____. An ICI fertiliser is named after the symbols for the three elements and is therefore called ____. Fertilisers are needed because of the rapid increase in world ____. Fertilisers do have at least one bad effect involving ____ levels in ____ water. Some experts feel that these levels of ____ can cause blue-____ syndrome and ____ cancer.

2 Fertilisers make ____ sense because yields of crops can be more than ____ for little outlay per hectare. Some experts think that ____ use of fertilisers can ruin the ____ of the soil.

3 ____ kill weeds and insecticides kill ____. Slugs and ____ are killed by ____, and eelworms are killed by ____. People who want crops untainted by ____ opt for produce from ____ farms. These farms only use ____ fertilisers and no ____ sprays. A modern pesticide has to be very ____ tested over a period of some ____ years since problems with ____ and 2,4,5,T.

4 Pest control in the future may involve ____ farms where natural ____ are specially ____ to attack pests. Microbes may be used to make ____ pesticides, yet another example of bio-____ making ____ chemicals. Bio-____ itself may mean less ____ crops will need to be ____.

INDEX

Acrylic plastic   70
Additives   72
Alcohol manufacture   54
Ammonia   2–5
Angina   29
Aspirin   28

Beta-blocker   29
Biodegradable plastic   72

Calcium carbonate   18–19
Calcium hydroxide   18
Calendering   71
Cement   20–21
Cement dust   22
Chemicals from coal   59–60
Chlor-alkali industry   11
Coal   58
Coal mine   59
Coal-powered cars   62
Concrete   19–20
Conductivity of heat   74–5
Contact process   6–7
Cracking   14
Crude oil contents   46

Destructive distillation   60
Detergent   13, 52
Drug development   29–32
Dye manufacture   37
Dyes   35

Economics of fertilisers   81
Elastomers   68
Electrolysis   11
Ethene   51, 69, 70
Extrusion   71

Fertilisers   77
Fertiliser problems   82
Fluidised-bed combustion   61
Foaming plastics   72
Fuels in the UK   58
Fungicides   86
Fractional distillation   47, 49

Glass   22–23
Glass-blowing   23–4
Granulation   78

Haber process   3–5
Heavy ash   14
Herbicides   84

Injection moulding   71
Insecticides   85

Light ash   15

Merseyside   8
Monomer   69, 70
Mossmorran pipeline   56–7

NGL pipeline   56–7
Nitric acid   5–6
Nitrogen in soil   79
North Sea oil/gas fields   44–5

Oil refinery   48
Oil well   42
Opium   27
Opren   33

Penicillin   28, 34
Pesticide manufacture   87–8
Pesticide sales   86
Pests   82
Petrol   55–6
Plastic   67
Polyethene   70
Propranolol   28–9
PVC   70
Pyrolysis   73

Recycling plastic   73
Reforming   51
Routes for soil nitrogen   79

Soap   12–13
Sodium carbonate   14–17
Sodium chloride   9–12
Solvay process   15–17
Sudan orange   37–8
Sulphuric acid   6–9
Superphosphate   77

Thermoplastic   68
Thermosetting plastic   68
Top ten drugs   33
Tremcard   2

Urea   77

World use of oil   53

ACKNOWLEDGEMENTS

The author would like to thank his wife Elizabeth and son Jonathan for their encouragement and support during the writing of this book.

The author and publishers are grateful to the following who provided photographs and gave permission for reproduction:

Shell UK Administrative Services (cover)
ICI Chemicals & Polymers Ltd; ICI Colours and Fine Chemicals (pp. 1, 9, 21, 37)
Blue Circle Industries PLC (p. 18)
Peter Keeling (pp. 20 (upper), 66, 69)
Thames Water (p. 20 (lower))
Coloroll Edinburgh Crystal (p. 23)
Roche Products Ltd (p. 27)
British Coal (pp. 59, 63)
Farmers Weekly (pp. 78, 83)

and to ICI Chemicals & Polymers Ltd for the TREMCARD on p. 2.

ANSWERS TO CROSSWORD (p. 24)

Across
2	Merseyside
8	Oral
9	Nitric
10	Odour
11	Sows
12	Oil
13	Haber
14	Nylons
15	Aga
19	Concrete
22	Ton
23	Ether
24	Ammonia
27	Ni
28	Saponification

Down
1	Runcorn
2	Metal
3	Success
4	Soda ash
5	Douse
6	Error
7	Glass
16	Acid rain
17	Tear
18	Contact
19	Canals
20	New map
21	ET
25	ICI
26	RIC
27	NO

ANSWERS TO CROSSWORD (p. 64)

Across
1	PVC
4	Alkanes
8	Reservoir
10	Roe
11	PTO
13	pH
14	Ear
16	Rig
19	OPEC
20	NGL
24	Fluidised bed
27	US
28	Reforming
31	Boom
32	Cyclo
34	Enzyme
35	Iran

Down
1	Perspex
2	Castor
3	Hard
5	North
6	Shell
7	Coke
9	Refined
12	TA
15	Aped
17	GG
18	He
21	Leek
22	Slurry
23	Bitumen
25	Use
26	Sum
29	File
30	Four
33	On